PREDATORS
THE WORLD'S DEADLIEST ANIMALS

PREDATORS
THE WORLD'S DEADLIEST ANIMALS

Paula Hammond

amber
BOOKS

Published by
Amber Books Ltd
United House
North Road
London N7 9DP
United Kingdom
www.amberbooks.co.uk
Instagram: amberbooksltd
Facebook: amberbooks
Twitter: @amberbooks

Project Editor: Sarah Uttridge
Design: Keren Harragan
Picture Research: Terry Forshaw

ISBN: 978-1-78274-973-8

Printed in China

Picture Credits
Alamy: 82 (Amazon Images), 114 (Rick & Nora Bowers), 152 (Graphic Science)
Corbis: 17R (JAI/Nigel Pavitt), 55L (Visuals Unlimited/Ken Catania), 75R (Royalty Free), 103R (Royalty Free)
Dreamstime: 16 (Aurell), 21L (Jumoku), 21R (Valentina 75), 25L (Andreanita), 25R (Mogens Trolle), 28 (Matthew G. Simpson), 29L (Morten Elm), 29R (Steffen Foerster), 33L (G Palms), 33R (Chris Lorenz), 36 (Daksel), 37L (Brian Sedgbeer), 37R (Lukas Blazek), 41L (Joan Egert), 41R (Neal Cooper), 46 (Erik Manore), 47R (Moose Henderson), 58 (Lajos Endredi), 62 (Lynn Bystrom), 63L (Charles T. Bennett), 66 (Paul Banton), 67L (Mazikab), 67R (Steffen Foerster), 71L (Hotshotsworldwide), 74 (Outdoorsman), 79L (Alexandre de Fagundes), 79R (Lukas Blazek), 87L (Franant), 94 (Rhallam), 107L (SWhite), 107R (Tamara Bauer), 110 (Alexander Shalamov), 111L (Alan0033), 111R (Edwin Verin), 119L (Ammit), 122 (Surz 01), 123L (Bernhard Richter), 130 (Christian Schmalhofer), 131L (Naturablichter), 131R (Mihail Zhukov), 134 (Smellme), 135L (Hotshotsworldwide), 135R (Crystal Taylor), 140 (Steve Dubois), 145L (Isselee), 148 (Mikhail Blajenov), 149L (Kathy Timmermann), 153R (Robert Gubiani), 157R (Nico Smit), 161R (Bernhard Richter), 165L (Dirk Ercken), 165R (Cathy Kiefer), 168 (Designpicssub), 173L (Brian Lasnby), 173R (Steve Byland), 177R (Fanny Reno), 181L (Outdoorsman), 184 (Maniel), 185L (Mgkuijpers), 189 both (Mathes)
FLPA: 12 (Tui de Roy), 13R (Pete Oxford), 17L (Jurgen & Christine Sohns), 24 (James Lowen), 32 (Tom Velo), 50 (Franz Christoph Robi), 51L (Gerard Lacz), 51R (Panda Photo), 54 (S, D & K Maslowski), 63R (Biosphoto/Guy Piton), 70 (Mitsuaki Iwago), 71R (Gerard Lacz), 75L (Paul Sawer), 78 (Kevin Shafer), 90-91 all (Biosphoto), 95L (Hiroya Minakuchi), 95R (Flip Nicklin), 98 (Gregory Guida), 99 both (Science Source), 103L (Paul Sawer), 115 both (Michael & Patricia Fogden), 126 (Dembinsky Photo), 127R (S, D & K Maslowski), 141L (Chien Lee), 141R (Michael & Patricia Fogden), 144, 145R (Imagebroker), 149R (Kurt Mobus), 156 (Imagebroker/Ingo Schulz), 157L & 160 & 161L (Michael & Patricia Fogden), 169 both (Thierry Montford), 172 (Albert Lleal), 176 (Frans Lanting), 177L (Mike Parry), 185R (Chris Mattison), 188 (Kevin Schafer)
Fotolia: 13L (D. Ho)
Getty Images: 127L (Peter Arnold)
Istock: 40 (Leezsnow), 106 (T-Immagini)
Photos.com: 20, 47L, 59 both, 86, 87R, 102, 118, 119R
Photoshot: 55R (Bruce Coleman/Dwight Kuhn), 83 both (NHPA/ANT), 153L (NHPA/Ken Griffiths)
Public Domain: 164
U.S. Fish & Wildlife Services: 123R, 180, 181R

Contents

Introduction

Imagine if a visitor from another planet asked you to describe what a predator looked like. Where would you begin? Perhaps you'd say that predators are big and fierce. That they have razor-sharp claws and powerful teeth—and you'd be partly right. However, predators come in all shapes and sizes, and some of them are very surprising indeed.

Predators are animals that hunt and eat other animals. Some, like the leopard, fit everyone's idea of what a predator should look like. But strength and raw power are not everything. Some predators, like the Cape cobra, don't have claws or teeth, but Mother Nature has given them something just as good: poison! Other predators don't seem to have any special advantages in the eat-or-be-eaten world. Unless, that is, you happen to be on the menu…

Take the African shoebill. These bizarre-looking birds spend their days lurking beside muddy swamps. When they do move they look as if they are in slow motion,

but don't be fooled! All this creeping around has a deadly purpose. To any creature in the water below, the shoebill doesn't look like a hunter; it looks just like a piece of floating vegetation. It is only when their prey comes within striking distance that these cunning carnivores strike. Moving with lightning speed, that comic-looking bill is suddenly transformed into a death trap, decapitating any creature within reach.

Then there's the grasshopper mouse. This furry little mammal couldn't look any cuter. Yet, in their own habitat, they are tiny terrors. They may have the body of mouse, but they have the heart and soul of a wolf. They even howl at the moon like wolves!

They say that you should never judge by appearances, and that is certainly true in the animal kingdom. Not every muscle-bound beast is a killer, and not every killer is a muscle-bound beast. In this book, we'll be looking at some of the world's biggest, fiercest, and most peculiar predators.

Birds

Birds can be found on all seven continents, from Africa's parched grasslands to Australasia's tropical rainforests. Around 10,000 bird species have been identified, and these incredible creatures have adapted to cope with whatever nature has thrown at them.

Around 60 species are landlubbers (live on land) and do not fly at all. Some use their wings to "fly" beneath the waves, just as effectively as they do in the air. Others spend their whole lives "on the wing," only ever landing to mate.

Of all the animals on our planet, it is this ability to fly that sets birds apart. Birds and bats are the only creatures to have mastered true flight and only birds do it with such style and grace.

Watching these astonishing aerial acrobats in flight is an awe-inspiring sight. However, flight is more that just a handy way of getting around. It gives birds a huge advantage when they are hunting. Every species has its own specialized wing design that is perfectly adapted to its lifestyle. Forest hunters such as hawks have short, broad, rounded wings, which are ideal for swerving in and out of thick foliage. Most owls hunt at night, so they have big, smooth feathers that allow them to fly almost silently. Seabirds, such the frigate bird, have long, sculpted wings for gliding and diving. All of these features help to make birds very successful predators— whatever their environment.

Harpy Eagle

Scientific Name: *Harpia harpyja*

HEAD
The head is covered by rows of large pale gray feathers. This creates a striking double crest that is raised whenever the bird is alarmed.

EYES
Dark brown or gray eyes are positioned at the front of the head. This gives the eagle "binocular" vision, which is perfect for judging distances.

FEATHERS
The upper body is covered with black feathers. Feathers on the eagle's underside are mostly white, except for a black band across the breast.

TALONS
Large feet and razor-sharp talons are used to grab prey and tear flesh. The talons can grow up to 5in (12.5cm) in length.

As it swoops through the trees, the harpy eagle (*Harpia harpyja*) strikes fear into the hearts of every rainforest animal. This imposing creature is one of the world's largest birds of prey and a top predator in its natural habitat. The harpy eagle lives in lowland rainforests, where food can literally be plucked from the trees—if, that is, you have the tools for the job! This impressive predator certainly does. Like all birds of prey, it has incredible eyesight. It can spot objects less than ¾in (2cm) long from almost 656ft (200m) away. Its wings are short, with rounded tips that help the bird maneuver through dense foliage. The bird's knife-like talons kill and dismember prey.

ACTUAL SIZE

▷ THIS MONKEY HAS EVERY REASON to be wary. Unlike many birds of prey, who soar high above the rainforest canopy looking for food, harpy eagles hunt in the forest itself. There they perch, silently and patiently, for hours at a time, waiting for unsuspecting animals to come just a bit too close. Then they strike! Their specialized wings allow them to not only swoop downward, very quickly, but fly almost straight up. This means they can attack prey from both below and above. These large eagles can kill almost any animal, but monkeys and sloths are their favorite food.

Where in the world?

Harpy eagles inhabit lowland South American rainforests, from Mexico to Argentina. Due to deforestation, these magnificent birds have all but vanished from most of Central America, although they are still found in parts of Panama.

Did you know?

• Harpy eagles are named after winged spirits from Greek mythology. The film *Jason and the Argonauts* tells a version of the story of Phineus the Seer, who was punished by the gods by being placed on an island with a buffet of food that the harpies always stole from him before he had the chance to eat.

• Fawkes the Phoenix in the series of *Harry Potter* movies was based on the harpy eagle.

• The talons of the harpy eagle are bigger than the claws of a North American grizzly bear!

• According to *The Guinness Book of Animal Facts and Feats*, the largest harpy eagle was a tame female called Jezebel, who weighed in at 27lb (12.2kg). That is almost twice the weight of a wild female harpy eagle.

PHOTOFILE: Harpy Eagle

▷ **Close to home**
Even after it has learned to fly, a juvenile harpy eagle stays close to home. It takes time to perfect the skills needed to survive, so the youngster remains with its parents for up to two years.

FACT

Believe it or not, this big, powerful bird is still just a baby! It takes up to six years for a harpy to fully mature. During its first year, its head, underside, and thigh feathers are white. By the time it is three, its head will be grayer and black bands will have started to appear on its thighs. It is only in its fourth year that the eagle's plumage starts to look like that of its parents.

△ Facial disc
Feathers around the eyes
form a "facial disc." In birds
of prey this is thought to
help focus sound. Owls have
very large facial discs. The
harpy's disc is smaller, but
does the same job.

▷ Vast nests
The harpy eagle nests in tall trees.
There, they build vast nests made from
a base of large sticks, lined with leaves.
The nest may be up to 164ft (50m) off
the ground.

Shoebill

Scientific Name: *Balaeniceps rex*

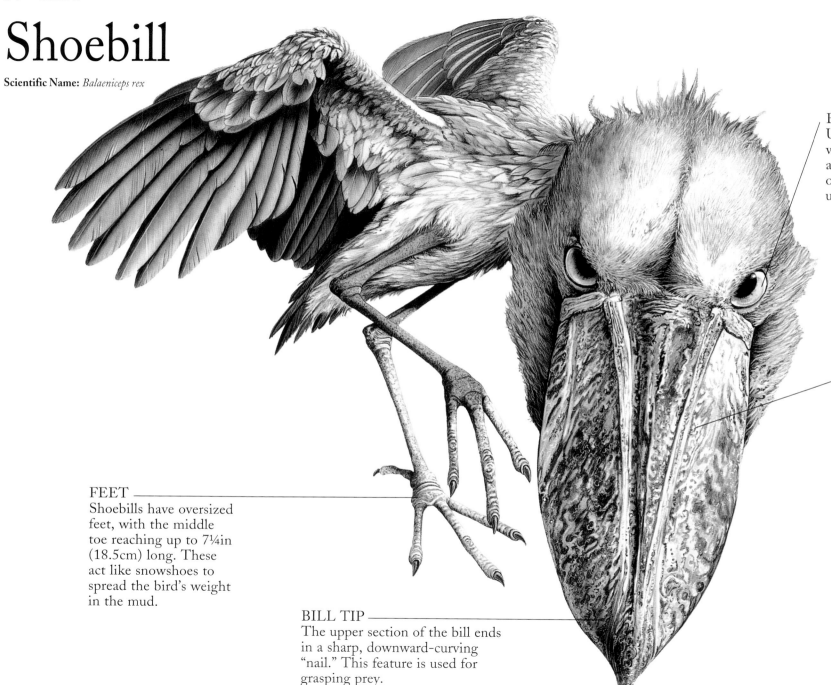

EYES
Unlike many wading birds, which use their feet to feel around in the water in search of prey, the shoebill hunts using its superb eyesight.

BILL
The large shoe-like bill is the most prominent feature of this well-named bird. It measures about 8in long by 8in around (20 by 20cm).

FEET
Shoebills have oversized feet, with the middle toe reaching up to 7¼in (18.5cm) long. These act like snowshoes to spread the bird's weight in the mud.

BILL TIP
The upper section of the bill ends in a sharp, downward-curving "nail." This feature is used for grasping prey.

The shoebill (*Balaeniceps rex*) doesn't exactly match the image that most people have of what a predator looks like. With its long, lanky legs, bulky body, and a head that looks like a dodo's, shoebills look funny rather than fierce. However, its comic appearance disguises the fact that this bird is really a very clever hunter. Shoebills live in Africa's tropical marshlands, where they prey on anything from lung fish to Nile monitors. That bizarre bill is its main weapon; the edges are so sharp that it can slice up small prey such as frogs and water snakes with ease. If anything bigger comes its way, then the shoebill simply flips open its massive mouth ready to crush and gulp down anything tasty.

ACTUAL SIZE

▷ THE SECRET TO THE SHOEBILL'S success is patience! These birds spend their days lurking on the edge of muddy swamps. When they do move, they look as if they are in slow motion. But all this creeping around has a deadly purpose. To the baby crocodile, below the water, the shoebill doesn't look like a hunter, just a shadow cast by vegetation. It is only when the crocodile comes up for air that this cunning carnivore attacks. Striking with lightning speed, that comic-looking bill is transformed into a death trap, and its sharp edges easily slice the poor crocodile in two.

Where in the world?

Shoebills are most at home around the freshwater marshes of tropical central Africa. They can be found in swampy areas, from the Sudan to Zambia, and occasionally wander into flooded farmland in search of food.

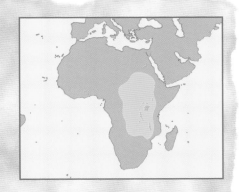

Did you know?

● Having such a big bill is handy for catching food, but it does have some disadvantages. When shoebills lunge forward to attack their prey, they have to hold their wings back so they don't lose their balance and topple over!

● Although this odd bird was only classified by European scientists in the 19th century, the birds were well known to ancient Egyptians. Drawings of the shoebill, dating from approximately 3500 BCE, appear on the walls of Egyptian tombs.

● When young shoebills are begging for food from their parents they make a sound very much like a human with hiccups!

● Arabs refer to the shoebill as *abu markub*. This translates as "one with a shoe," in reference to the bird's prominent and very strange-shaped bill.

PHOTOFILE: Shoebill

▷ **Falling population**
Worldwide, the shoebill population is falling rapidly. There are many reasons for this. Habitat destruction is a major factor, as swamps are drained so that the land can be used for farming or building.

FACT

Shoebills spend their lives in and around water. During the breeding season they even build floating nests! They start by constructing a platform, which can be up to 10ft (3m) across. On top of this they pile broken reeds, sticks, and foliage to create their very own floating island. This helps protect their eggs from land-bound predators and also allows them to feed their chicks without leaving the nest for too long.

△ **Mooing noises**
Generally shoebills are a
silent species, but during the
breeding season, adults
clatter their bills and make
odd, moo-like calls. These
calls are thought to help the
pair bond and are copied by
the young hatchlings.

▷ **Startled shoebill**
If a shoebill is startled, it will take to the
air, usually flying low over the water,
and not very far. It can also use its broad
wings to soar high on warm air currents.

Barn Owl

Scientific Name: Genus *Tyto*

EARS
The owl's left ear is higher than the right and points downward. The right ear points slightly up. This helps the owl "tune in" on its prey.

EYES
A barn owl's eyes are around twice as sensitive to light as human eyes. This means that it can see quite well in the dark.

TALONS
Owl's feet are zygodactyl; this means that two toes face forward and two face backward. This "design" is common for birds that perch or live in trees.

LEGS & FEET
Compared to other owls, barn owls have long legs, toes, and talons. This allows them to catch prey even if it is hiding amid deep foliage.

The barn owl (genus *Tyto*) is a born predator. Every inch of this incredible creature is designed to make it the perfect hunter. Those long wings are made for slow flight, allowing the owl take its time pinpointing prey. A soft fringe of feathers on the leading edge of each wing means that it can fly in complete silence. Although the barn owl has superb eyesight, it can hunt in total darkness too thanks to its super-sensitive hearing. In fact, that curious heart-shaped face works a little like a sonar dish, funneling sound toward the owl's ears. Add a pair of long talons, which can grab prey even when it is hidden deep under vegetation, and the result is a silent and deadly killer.

ACTUAL SIZE

▷ HAVE YOU EVER SEEN a cartoon ghost? The type that looks like a white sheet, with holes for eyes and its arms outstretched, gliding just above the ground. That popular image owes much to the hunting habits of the barn owl! Unlike tawny owls, barn owls don't hoot, they shriek. Combine that with a pale face, black eyes, long outstretched wings, and a habit of gliding silently around in the dark, and you have a ready-made ghost! Unfortunately for this little mouse, though, this is no ghostly apparition. The danger is all too real—and getting closer by the minute.

Where in the world?

It is believed that there are around 20–30 subspecies of barn owls. These adaptable birds are found all over the world, although they avoid desert and Arctic regions. They like open countryside, near farms or woods.

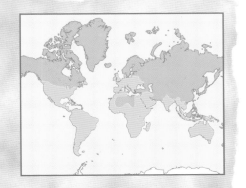

Did you know?

● As owls don't have teeth, they have to swallow their food whole. Any indigestible parts such as bones, claws, or fur are regurgitated (coughed up) later in the form of a neat little pellet.

● The barn owl's eyes are fixed in position. If it wants to look to either side or behind, it just swivels its head round. In fact, owls can move their head up to 270 degrees in any direction!

● On average, a barn owl catches and eats four small mammals every night. That's 1,460 a year!

● While hunting, one of the barn owl's back toes swivels round to face forward. Barn owls kill their prey by squeezing it, so this allows the bird to exert more pressure on the body of its captives.

PHOTOFILE: Barn Owl

▷ **Detecting sound**
Hearing is a very important tool in the barn owl's arsenal. This is why they usually hunt no more than a few feet above the ground. At this height, the owl can detect the slightest sound.

FACT

Barn owls are nocturnal. They hunt under cover of darkness, but can sometimes be spotted flying slowly back and forth in search of prey. This is called quartering. Barn owl usually hunt "on the wing," but sometimes they will sit on a convenient perch, scanning for prey before swooping down to catch it. As they do so, they push out their legs. This both slows them down and positions their talons ready to grab their victim.

△ **Fluffy babies**
Baby barn owls (called owlets) begin flying at about eight weeks. At that age, their plumage (feathers) still looks quite fluffy. By ten weeks old, they will have lost that fluff and will look like an adult.

▷ **Nesting inside**
In the UK, barn owls usually nest inside buildings or holes in trees or rock faces. The owl's plumage contains very little oil to keep out water, so they prefer to roost inside where it's dry!

Brown Skua

Scientific Name: *Stercorarius antarcticus* also *Catharacta antarctica*

WINGS
Large, strong wings help to make the skua fast, acrobatic fliers. This ability is very useful when it is hunting or harrying other birds for food.

BODY
On average, the brown skua measures about 2ft (60cm) in the body and has a wingspan of around 4ft (1.2m).

BILL TIP
Brown skuas look a little like large, dark gulls. The key to identifying them is a fleshy structure called a cere, which is found on the upper mandible.

BILL
All birds' bills are made up of two jaws. These are generally called the upper mandible (or maxilla) and the lower mandible (or mandible).

The brown skua (*Stercorarius antarcticus*, also *Catharacta antarctica*) is a real pirate of the bird world. Although these very aggressive birds generally prey on penguin colonies, they see no reason to give up the chance of an easy meal. Skua are such skillful fliers that they will often harass other birds in the air, pulling at its wings and tail until it either drops its own catch or disgorges (throws up) the meal it has just eaten. If the bird is lucky, that will distract the skua long enough for it to make a clean getaway. If it is unlucky, the bird may find itself on the menu too! Skua will often kill and eat other seabirds including shags, terns, petrels, and gulls.

ACTUAL SIZE

▷ SKUAS ARE NOT PARTICULARLY FUSSY eaters. If they have the chance, they will even pick up scraps dropped overboard by fishing boats. However, their favorite foods are penguin chicks and eggs. Usually skuas are solitary hunters, but in the breeding season, when they have their own chicks to feed, they will work as a team. One bird will distract the penguin parents while the other steals in to take what it can. If a chick is small, the skua may swallow it whole. Larger chicks, however, need more work, and that is where that wicked-looking hook on the tip of the skua's bill comes in useful.

Where in the world?

Brown skuas are found on the Antarctic Peninsula and sub-Antarctic islands like South Georgia and the Falklands. They prefer habitats occupied by ground-nesting seabirds or penguins, but will move further north outside the breeding season.

Did you know?

● Life in a skua colony is a life of constant conflict. These birds are famously argumentative and are unable to get along even with members of their own species. Even bird watchers who get just a little too close to a nesting skua can expect to be driven off with bill and claw!

● In one well-known study, a single skua couple were discovered to have eaten more than 1,000 eggs during the penguin's breeding season.

● A survey in 2009 found an egg of a macaroni penguin being incubated in a skua's nest. It is thought that the egg was dropped there by accident and, once it was in the nest, the female no longer saw it as food, but as one of her own eggs!

Brown Skua

▷ **Hunting and breeding**
Brown skua are found further south than any other flying bird, apart from polar skua. These widely traveled birds can spend seven months a year hunting, but return to their breeding sites in late October to mate.

FACT

Although they spend most of their year apart, scouring the oceans in search of food, brown skuas mate for life. Once they return to their nesting site, they greet their mate with a series of long calls and a wing raising display that helps the pair to bond again. If the female skua cannot find her mate from the previous year, she will usually try to find another partner or even breed with a polar skua.

△ **Begging for food**
As young birds mature, their
parents gradually feed them
less and less to encourage
them to hunt for themselves.
However, when they are hungry
they will still noisily beg one of
their parents for food.

▷ **Hah-hah-hah-hah cry**
Many members of the skua family look
similar, but they can be recognized by their
calls. The brown skua has a very distinctive
and harsh hah-hah-hah-hah cry. They also
have special alarm and recognition calls.

Frigate bird

Scientific Name: Genus *Fregata*

WINGS
The frigate bird's enormous wings enable it to fly for very long periods with little effort. A male's wingspan can measure up to 8ft (2.4m).

TAIL
A tail gives a bird balance and aids its agility in the air. The frigate bird's long, forked tail allows it to twist and turn in flight.

FEET
All four toes on the frigate bird's feet are webbed. This is a common adaptation for seabirds, although the frigate's webbing is less pronounced.

GULAR POUCH
Male frigate birds have a bright red throat pouch, called a gular pouch, which they inflate to attract females during the mating season.

The frigate bird (genus *Fregata*) is one of nature's true specialists. This amazing creature spends almost its entire life flying. In fact, it can stay airborne for up to a week, stopping only to roost during the mating season! Although most seabirds hunt by diving into the water in pursuit of prey, the frigate bird cannot swim. However, that is no problem for this magnificent aerial acrobat. It hunts by flying low over the water. When prey is in sight, it drops downs with incredible speed. Using that long hooked bill it is able to pluck fish, crustaceans, and even small sea turtles out of the water without so much as a pause. It is a technique that needs skill and daring—one error can be fatal.

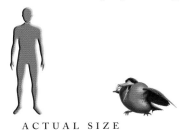

ACTUAL SIZE

▷ THIS BOOBIE HAS BEEN BUSY hunting all morning. Unfortunately, its success has attracted some unwanted attention. Frigate birds are also known as Man-o'-War birds. The name comes from a type of 16th-century warship that was popular with pirates. Grasping the boobie by the tail, these bullies harass their victim until, finally, it drops its catch. Fortunately for the boobie, such behavior is relatively rare; it usually happens only during the breeding season, when there are extra mouths to feed. Most of the time frigates are happy plucking fish from the water or flying fish from the air!

Where in the world?

Frigate birds occupy tropical waters, mostly the Pacific, but occasionally the Indian and Atlantic oceans. The Ascension frigate bird breeds only on Boatswain Bird Island, off the Ascension Islands. The Christmas frigate bird is endemic to that island.

Did you know?

● A favorite food of the magnificent frigate bird is flying fish. Flying fish can leap out of the water and use their long, wing-like fins to glide. They usually do this to escape predators like dolphins, but often end up in the belly of a frigate bird instead!

● Young frigate birds drop items like feathers in mid-air and practice catching them in preparation for the time when they are old enough to hunt for themselves.

● The frigate bird has the largest wingspan-to-body size of any bird. Of the five known species, the magnificent frigate bird is the largest, while the least frigate bird is the smallest.

● Frigate birds glide on warm tropical updrafts. Sometimes they ride weather fronts, and their appearance is believed to signal a change in the weather.

PHOTOFILE: Frigate bird

▷ **Gliding on the Wind**
Frigate birds fly fairly slowly, continuously climbing then descending (moving down), to glide on the trade winds. The only other species of bird that is known to spend the night "on the wing" like the frigate bird is the swift.

FACT
Frigate birds rely on underwater predators such as dolphins to force fish up to the ocean's surface. This is a fairly rare occurrence, so it is important for their survival that they use as little energy as possible while hunting. These amazing birds are designed for an aerial life and have the largest wing-area-to-body mass of any bird. This allows them to spend their days and nights in the air without spending too much energy.

△ **Inflatable pouch**
The frigate bird's gular pouch
takes up to 20 minutes to fully
inflate; the finished effect is very
dramatic. In other species, such as
pelicans, the pouch makes a handy
place to store food while hunting.

▷ **Mating season**
During the mating season, many male
birds undergo a dramatic transformation.
They shed their winter feathers for brighter,
bolder-colored mating plumage. Similarly,
the frigate bird's gular pouch only turns
bright red for the breeding season.

Western Screech Owl

Scientific Name: *Megascops kennicottii*

HEAD
The western screech owl flies with its head tucked in. This gives the bird a short and stubby outline, which is easy to identify.

EYES
Owls have the most forward-facing eyes of any species of bird. This gives them excellent binocular vision, which is vital for judging distances correctly.

PLUMAGE
Screech owls are polymorphic, meaning they come in different colors. Their plumage can be gray or reddish-brown (rufus). Red is more common in the south.

BODY
Screech owls live in trees the same color as their plumage. This natural camouflage makes them almost impossible to see unless you know they're there!

The western screech owl (*Megascops kennicottii*) lives mainly on insects, small mammals, and other birds. This may not sound that impressive, but before you dismiss this little predator's hunting prowess, think for a moment. Imagine trying to catch a moth while you are flying through a tangled forest in the dark. Or plucking up a mouse in the undergrowth that you have only heard and not seen. Or scooping a crayfish off the surface of the water, without even getting your feet wet. Screech owls can do all of this and more. Like all owls, the screech owl is a skilled and agile flyer. Its eyesight is superb, while its bill and feet are prefect for catching, holding, and killing prey quickly and efficiently.

ACTUAL SIZE

▷ THESE SMALL, AGILE BIRDS of prey make their homes in North American woodlands. They even venture into parks and gardens, although, being nocturnal, they are very hard to spot. Their preferred method of hunting is to wait patiently while hunkered down on a convenient perch. Like most owls, they hunt at dawn and dusk when their natural abilities really come into their own. Screech owls store any uneaten prey in holes. Sometimes, if a male is looking for a mate, he may even keep several "stores" full of tempting goodies in the hope of winning over a female.

Where in the world?

Western screech owls can be found from British Columbia to Texas. They like open woodlands and the edges of forest clearings beside rivers. They will venture into parks and gardens if the hunting is good.

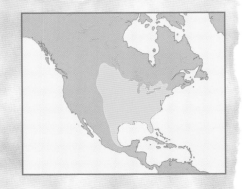

Did you know?

● The odd name, screech owl, comes from the unearthly and piercing calls produced by these lovely little owls. There are 21 different subspecies of screech owl and their calls all sound a little different.

● A poem written by Lady Mary Wortley Montagu (1689-1762) evokes the unearthly screams of the screech owl: "The screech-owl, with ill-boding cry, Portends strange things, old women say; Stops every fool that passes by, And frights the schoolboy from his play."

● In Texas, screech owls have been known to place blind snakes in their nests. The snakes are harmless to the owlets, but act like maids, keeping the nest clean!

● As is often the case with birds of prey, female screech owls tend to be larger than the males of the species.

PHOTOFILE: Western Screech Owl

▷ **Fierce Little Hunter**
The western screech owl is no bigger than 9in (23cm). However, this small owl is a fierce predator and will often catch animals much larger, relative to its size, than the prey of other owls.

FACT

Screech owls are generally opportunist hunters that take whatever food is available, depending on the season. During the breeding season, the female stays with the chicks for their first few weeks of life, while her mate brings home food for the whole family. At about five weeks, when the chicks are more independent, both parents will start to hunt to ensure that there is enough prey to keep the rapidly growing owlets strong and healthy.

△ **Scary eye tufts**
These owls raise their eye
tufts when they are alarmed
and want to make themselves
look bigger and scarier to
predators. In this instance,
though, it only manages to
make the owl look even cuter!

▷ **Owl in disguise**
The western screech owl is a master
of disguise. When alarmed, the owl
stretches its body, tightens its feathers,
and freezes. So, to the casual observer it
looks like part of the tree it is perched in.

Southern Ground Hornbill

Scientific Name: *Bucorvus leadbeateri*

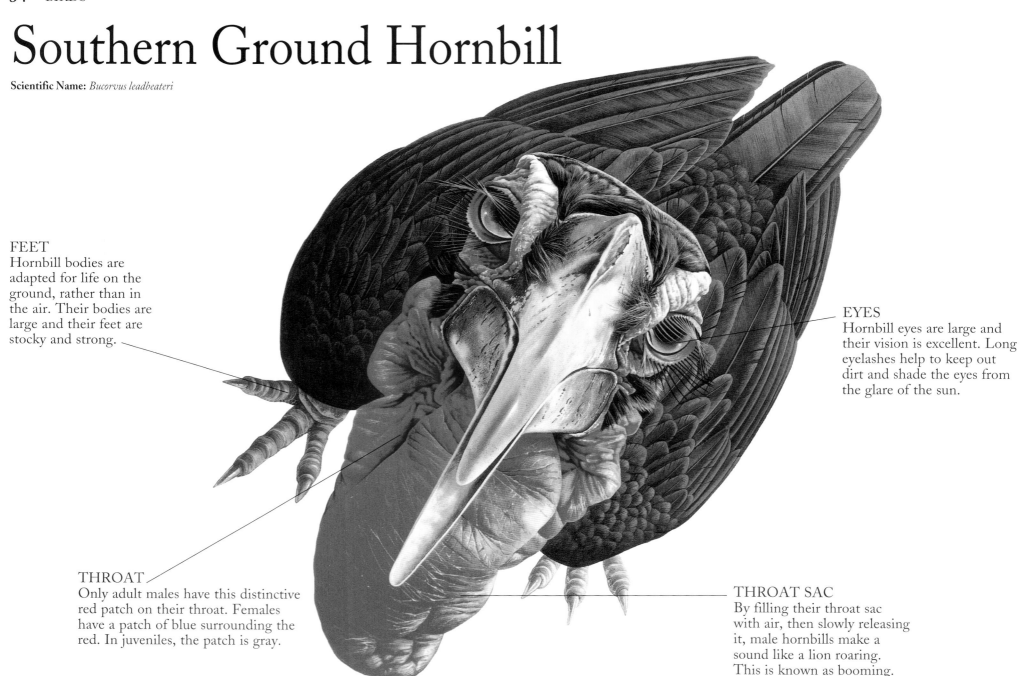

FEET
Hornbill bodies are adapted for life on the ground, rather than in the air. Their bodies are large and their feet are stocky and strong.

EYES
Hornbill eyes are large and their vision is excellent. Long eyelashes help to keep out dirt and shade the eyes from the glare of the sun.

THROAT
Only adult males have this distinctive red patch on their throat. Females have a patch of blue surrounding the red. In juveniles, the patch is gray.

THROAT SAC
By filling their throat sac with air, then slowly releasing it, male hornbills make a sound like a lion roaring. This is known as booming.

For a bird as big as a turkey, southern ground hornbills (*Bucorvus leadbeateri*) are surprisingly graceful. That huge dagger-like bill isn't just used for stabbing and grabbing, although it's very good at that! The tip can be used with great precision, like fingers, to pluck insects from the air. And if there is something tasty just beneath the ground, then it doubles as a very handy spade to root out grubs, reptiles, and small mammals. However, the real secret to the hornbill's success as a hunter lies in teamwork. Hornbills live in family groups and, what they lack in teeth and claws, they more than make up for in group aggression. Working together, they'll even take on prey as big as hares or as deadly as cobras.

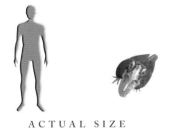

ACTUAL SIZE

▷ SOUTHERN GROUND HORNBILLS live in family groups, where one mating pair (usually the biggest male and female) is helped by the rest of the flock. They don't breed every year, and only lay two or three eggs at a time, so it is important for the the group's survival that the breeding pair has plenty of help. The family occupies a territory of up to 39 square miles (100 sq km) and will defend it aggressively, as this visitor has just found out. Although they are large birds, and more at home on the ground, they can fly when the family is at risk.

Did you know?

● The hornbill's bill is so heavy that the first two vertebrae (neck bones) are fused together for added strength.

● Male hornbills gather food in their bills to take back to the nesting female. If they spot anything tasty to add to their haul, they lay all their food on the ground in a neat line. Once they have added their new catch to the store, they sort the food and pick up all the pieces again.

● The hornbill's eyelashes are modified feathers.

● Hornbills react aggressively to anything that enters their territory; they often even attack their own reflections in windows!

● As southern ground hornbills only raise one chick at a time, conservationists collect any hatchlings that have been left to starve. These are raised by hand and released into the wild.

Where in the world?

Southern ground hornbills are found in southern Africa, ranging from southern Kenya down into South Africa. Their ideal hunting grounds are grassland savannahs, although they are occasionally found in the forests of eastern Africa.

PHOTOFILE: Southern Ground Hornbill

▷ **Hornbill Coloring**
Juvenile hornbills have duller, browner feathers and lack the red throat patch. This makes them less obvious to potential predators. They finally get their adult plumage and coloring (opposite) at around four years of age.

FACT

The "bump" on top of the hornbill's long, curved bill is called a casque. The casque is a hollow structure made out of the same material as nails and hair (keratin). It is believed that the casque acts like an echo chamber to make the hornbill's call sound louder. The casque on the male hornbill is generally larger than that on the female, probably because the male relies on its loud calls to attract mates and to defend its territory.

△ Safety in the trees
At night, hornbills take to the
treetops for safety to roost.
During the breeding season,
they make permanent nests in
large, natural cavities in trees
and sometimes rock faces,
which they line with leaves.

▷ Walking birds
As their name suggests, ground hornbills are
most at home on the ground. They spend
their days walking at a slow, ponderous pace,
searching the ground for prey. Anything warm
and wriggling is potential food!

Martial Eagle

Scientific Name: *Polemaetus bellicosus*

EYES
In common with all birds of prey, martial eagles have extremely good eyesight. In fact, their eyes are 3.6 times more sensitive than a human's.

WINGS
Big, broad wings are the ideal design for soaring. Long, finger-like primary feathers on each wing tip give the eagle greater control in the air.

TALONS
Sharp talons are used to hold down and kill prey. These are held outstretched, when the eagle is in the air, ready to grab prey.

LEGS
Tearing up prey can be messy. Many birds of prey have fewer feathers on their legs so their plumage doesn't get matted with blood.

The largest eagle in Africa spends much of its time circling its territory, looking for food. As it soars, high in the air, it may look to prey on the ground, below, like a tiny dot in the distance. However, martial eagles (*Polemaetus bellicosus*) have superb eyesight; even if you can't see them, they can certainly see you! These magnificent hunters are able to spot prey up to 3 miles (4.8km) away. When they do, they react with lightning speed, going into a slanting, high-speed dive called a stoop.

ACTUAL SIZE

Around half of their prey consists of other birds, including Egyptian geese that are as big as the eagle itself. The rest of its diet is made up of mammals and reptiles, including some of Africa's most poisonous snakes.

▷ "MARTIAL" MEANS "WAR-LIKE" or "soldierly," and this eagle is certainly living up to its name! Although these fearsome hunters are known to prey on farm animals like goats, it is unlikely that he really intends to eat this warthog. It is the breeding season and even though the hog isn't a threat to his chick, the eagle is taking no chances. Martial eagles only lay one egg every two years and it can take 12 months before the fledgling is big enough to fend for itself. During this time, both parents will react aggressively to anything that enters their territory while the chick is nesting.

Where in the world?

Martial eagles are found in sub-Saharan Africa, from Senegal to South Africa. They prefer open grasslands, semi-desert, and thornbush regions. They are not found in the forests of the Congo—the crowned eagle is king there.

Did you know?

● It has been said that these beautiful birds are so powerful they can break a human's arm with one blow from their feet!

● Thanks to their size and power, martial eagles are one of Africa's "apex" (top) bird predators. Worldwide, the martial eagle is the fifth largest eagle. It measures up to 3ft (90cm) in length, and has a wingspan up to 8ft 6in (2.5m) long.

● In the creation myths of the Boshongo people of Africa, the world began when god vomited up nine animals. These included the leopard, the eagle, and the crocodile.

● One of the biggest threats to the survival of the martial eagle is persecution from farmers. Eagles are seen as a threat to livestock, so they are often trapped, shot, or poisoned.

PHOTOFILE: Martial Eagle

▷ **Perch and Pounce**
Martial eagles mostly hunt from the air, circling their territory in search of prey. Occasionally they use the "perch and pounce" technique, using a perch to spot potential prey, before making a kill.

FACT

An eagle's nest is called an eyrie. Martial eagle nests are huge structures made from layers of sticks lined with leaves. These are either built high up, in the fork of a tree, or on a cliff top. A newly built nest can measure 5ft (1.5m) in diameter and be more than 2ft (60cm) deep. The eagle couple will reuse the nest year after year, and will enlarge it regularly.

△ Eagle coloring
Adult martial eagles have dark upper parts and whitish underparts, speckled with black spots. Juvenile birds are paler brown with fewer spots. They develop their adult plumage at around seven years of age.

▷ Wing tips
The finger-like tips on the eagle's wings increase lift and reduce drag without increasing the overall size of the wing surface. Modern passenger airlines have winglets on their wing tips that do a similar job.

Mammals

Mammals come in all shapes and sizes. They can be furry, prickly, or covered in scales. Some of them live underground, and some of them fly. Some make their homes on the icy fringes of the Arctic Circle, while others prefer the dry, baking heat of the desert.

Since mammals first appeared on our planet, around 210 million years ago, these tenacious and adaptable creatures have evolved to inhabit almost every corner of the Earth. They have even been sent into outer space! Albert II, a Rhesus monkey, became the first mammal to leave the atmosphere in 1949, when he was sent up in an American V2 rocket.

Yet, for all their wonderful variety and complexity, all land-dwelling, predatory mammals have one thing in common: they are carnivorous, which means they have a taste for meat! And it is that all-important need to feed that has made mammals some of the most successful—and the most notorious—hunters on the planet.

In this chapter you will meet two of the world's biggest and baddest predators: the Siberian tiger, and the infamous polar bear. Both species sit at the very top of the food chain and have, on occasion, even put another great predator, humans, on the menu!

However, for every large and powerful predator there are many more, like the star nosed mole, the echidna, and the ghost bat, which, despite their modest size, are such skilled hunters that they are still king of all they survey.

Wolverine

Scientific Name: *Gulo gulo*

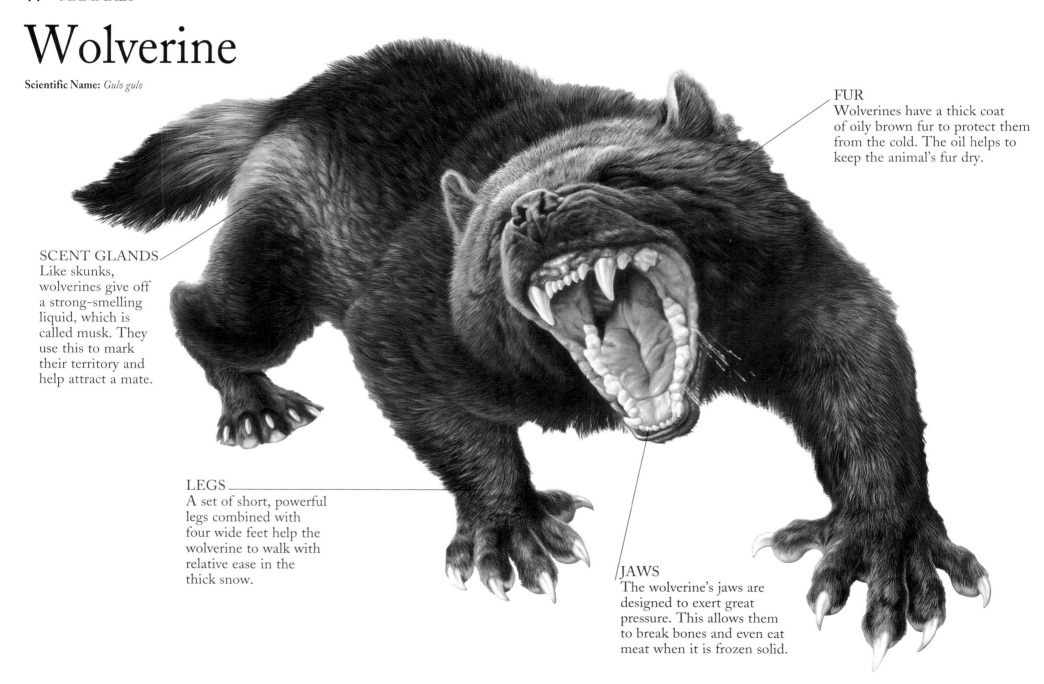

FUR
Wolverines have a thick coat of oily brown fur to protect them from the cold. The oil helps to keep the animal's fur dry.

SCENT GLANDS
Like skunks, wolverines give off a strong-smelling liquid, which is called musk. They use this to mark their territory and help attract a mate.

LEGS
A set of short, powerful legs combined with four wide feet help the wolverine to walk with relative ease in the thick snow.

JAWS
The wolverine's jaws are designed to exert great pressure. This allows them to break bones and even eat meat when it is frozen solid.

Anyone familiar with Marvel Comics' Wolverine will know that although he's short and stocky, he has massive claws and an attitude to match! The real-life wolverine (*Gulu gulu*) is just as awe-inspiring, with a reputation out of all proportion to its size. Most of the time it's content to prey on small mammals such as mice and rabbits. However, when the cold starts to bite this powerful predator shows its true prowess. This amazing animal is built like a bear cub, with dagger-like

ACTUAL SIZE

talons and powerful jaws. It may be small (similar to a medium-sized dog), but it is a fearless hunter. A wolverine will tackle prey ten times its own size. It has even been seen chasing bears away from fresh kills!

▷ EVEN IN WINTER, when food is scarce, sniffing out prey is no problem for the wolverine. Equipped with an acute sense of smell, this hungry hunter tracks down a lone moose trapped in the deep snow. Luckily for the wolverine, its wide feet work like snowshoes, allowing it to run where other animals would stumble and fall. Once trapped, the moose is doomed. Sinking its long, curved claws into its victim, the wolverine holds on until the moose dies of exhaustion and blood loss. Powerful jaws mean the wolverine makes quick work of its prey.

Where in the world?

Wolverines are found in cut off regions of the Arctic Circle, Europe and, northern north America. They can travel up to 15 miles (24km) a day, and need lots of space to hunt in.

Did you know?

● Wolverines may look like miniature bears, but they belong to the weasel family (*Mustelidae*). In fact, they are the largest land-dwelling mustelid. The Amazonian giant otter is the largest aquatic member of the weasel family.

● Inside that formidable jaw, the wolverine has 38 very sharp teeth. It has five partially retractable, sharp claws on each paw.

● European settlers called the wolverine the glutton because of the huge amount of food it is able to eat in one sitting. The wolverine's scientific name, *Gulo gulo*, is Latin for glutton.

● In Native American myths, the wolverine is a trickster-hero of the spiritual world.

● Female wolverines give birth about once every three years. The newborn babies are known as kits and the female will usually have a litter of two to three at a time.

PHOTOFILE: Wolverine

▷ **Climbing predator**
Wolverines are expert climbers, using their claws to get a good grip on tree bark. They use the extra height to help pinpoint prey, but occasionally they will pounce on their victim from this elevated vantage point.

FACT

In 1925, wildlife illustrator Ernest Thompson Seton described the wolverine like this: "Picture a weasel ... that symbol of slaughter, sleeplessness, and tireless, incredible activity ... multiply that mite some 50 times, and you have the likeness of a Wolverine." He went on: "The wolverine is ... a personality of unmeasured force, courage and achievement, but so enveloped in mists of legend ... fear and hatred that one scarcely knows ... what to accept as fact." (*From Lives of Game Animals Volume II*)

△ Stinky bear
Like most members of the
mustelid group, these
magnificent mammals give off
a powerful stench, known as
musk. The pungent odor that the
wolverine produces has earned it
the nicknames of skunk bear and
stink bear!

▷ Body and fur
The wolverine has a stocky body with
powerful limbs, a short tail, round head,
and small ears. Its fur is thick and long,
brownish-black in color with lighter
markings along the sides.

Greater Horseshoe Bat

Scientific Name: *Rhinolophus ferrumequinum*

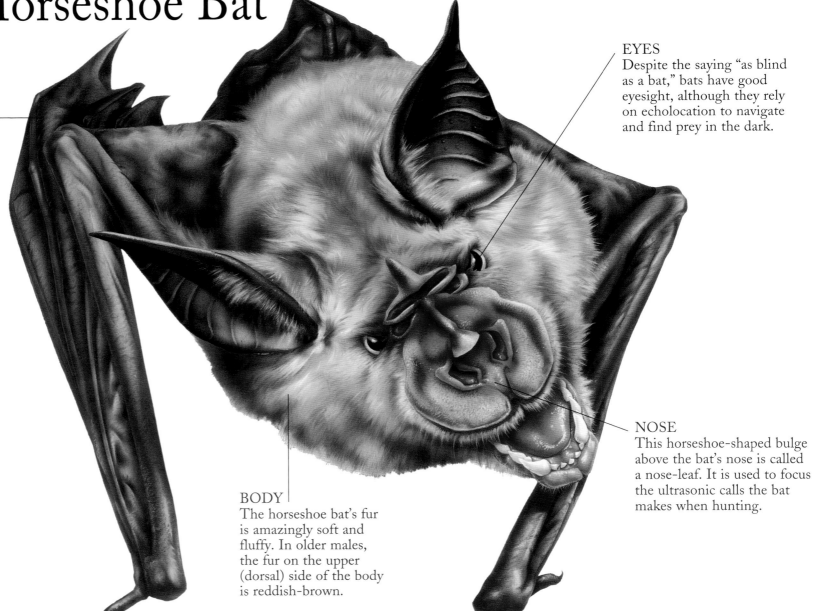

WINGS
Bats' wings do not have feathers. Instead, the wings are made up of a membrane of skin that is stretched across a set of massively elongated fingers.

EYES
Despite the saying "as blind as a bat," bats have good eyesight, although they rely on echolocation to navigate and find prey in the dark.

NOSE
This horseshoe-shaped bulge above the bat's nose is called a nose-leaf. It is used to focus the ultrasonic calls the bat makes when hunting.

BODY
The horseshoe bat's fur is amazingly soft and fluffy. In older males, the fur on the upper (dorsal) side of the body is reddish-brown.

very predator has something that gives them the edge over the animals they prey on. Sometimes it is just a matter of being bigger and stronger than the other guy. Some predators are team players, working in packs to overcome animals that they could never subdue single-handedly. There are some predators, though, whose success is due to very special abilities—and bats have not one, but two! Bats are the only mammal that can truly fly, which gives them a huge advantage when hunting. However, as they mostly hunt at night, horseshoe bats (*Rhinolophus ferrumequinum*) have another ability called echolocation. This works like sonar to help the bat find its way around in the dark.

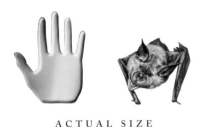

ACTUAL SIZE

▷ HUNTING AT NIGHT has great advantages. Your prey can't see you and you can't be seen by other, bigger predators. The only problem is, how can you hunt when you don't know where anything is? Horseshoe bats have a solution to this problem, called echolocation. Horseshoe bats generate a very high-pitched sound through their nose. When this sound hits an object, the bat uses the echo that bounces back to build up a picture of where things are. The system is so sensitive that a horseshoe bat has no trouble catching this cockchafer in flight.

Where in the world?

Greater horseshoe bats can be found across Europe, Asia, and northern north Africa. They usually roost in caves, but occasionally nest in the attics of houses. Their ideal homes are close to farmland and open water.

Did you know?

● Female horseshoe bats give birth hanging upside down, with their wings wrapped snugly around them. This allows the newborn baby bat (called a pup) to fall safely into its mother's overlapped wings.

● Bats make up around 20 percent of all known mammal species. The majority are insectivores (insect eaters) but there are bats that eat fruit (called frugivores), fish, and even vampire bats that, just like the fictional vampires, drink blood!

● Horseshoe bats belong to a group known as microbats. All members of the microbat family use echolocation to hunt. Most megabats do not.

● The ability to fly has allowed bats to spread to almost every part of our planet. With the exception of the Arctic, the Antarctic, and a few islands, bats can be found all over the world.

PHOTOFILE: Greater Horseshoe Bat

▷ **Hunting on the wing**
Most prey is captured in flight, but occasionally the horseshoe bat will hunt from a perch. Smaller insects can be eaten on the wing too, while larger prey is taken to a suitable site to consume.

FACT

If you look at your hands, you will see small flaps of skin at the base of each finger. Bat wings are really just elongated fingers, with a much larger and tougher membrane of skin stretched between them (called a patagium). When the muscles in a bat's "arm" flex, the patagium flips open like an umbrella. The smaller interfemoral membrane joins the bat's back legs together. This helps the bat brake and change direction in the air.

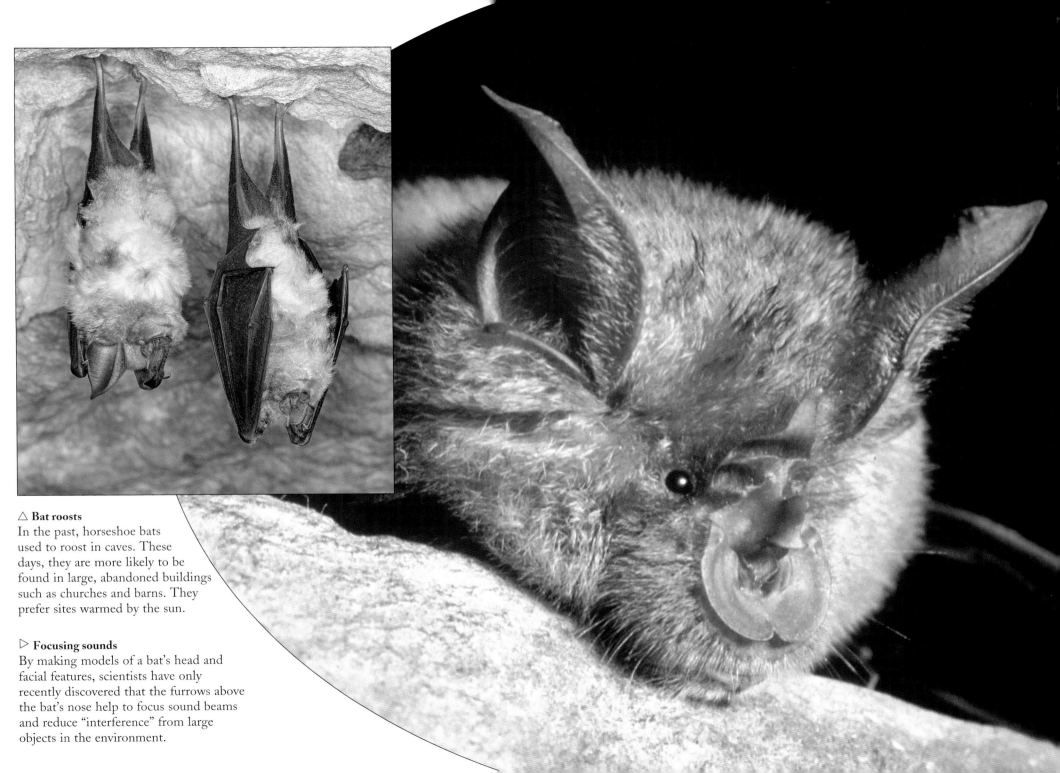

△ **Bat roosts**
In the past, horseshoe bats used to roost in caves. These days, they are more likely to be found in large, abandoned buildings such as churches and barns. They prefer sites warmed by the sun.

▷ **Focusing sounds**
By making models of a bat's head and facial features, scientists have only recently discovered that the furrows above the bat's nose help to focus sound beams and reduce "interference" from large objects in the environment.

Star-nosed Mole

Scientific Name: *Condylura cristata*

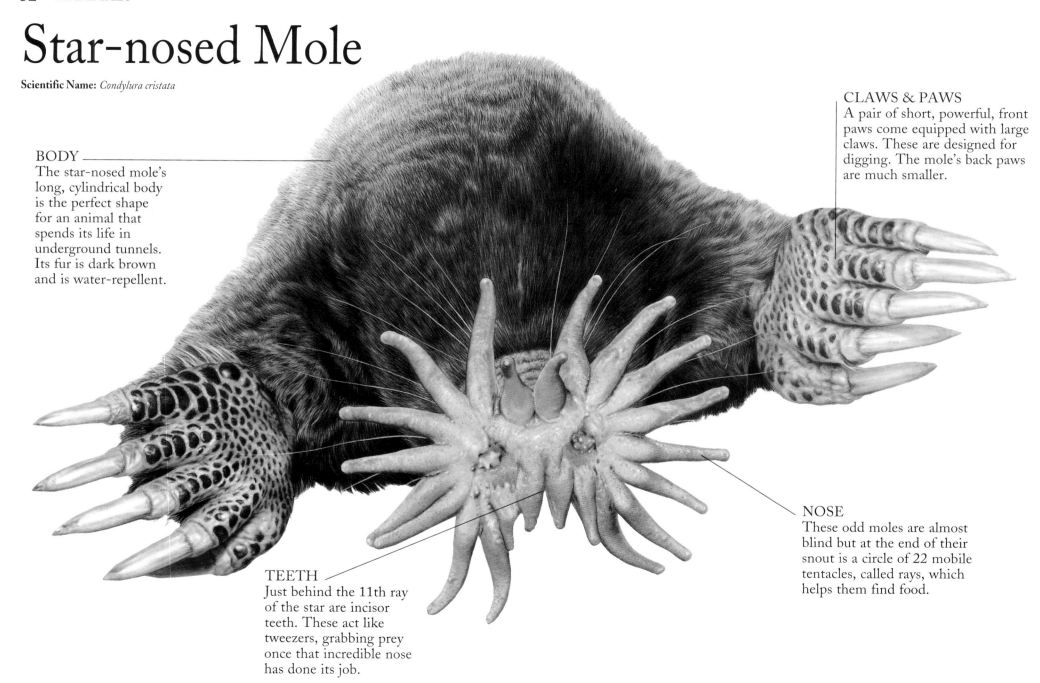

BODY
The star-nosed mole's long, cylindrical body is the perfect shape for an animal that spends its life in underground tunnels. Its fur is dark brown and is water-repellent.

CLAWS & PAWS
A pair of short, powerful, front paws come equipped with large claws. These are designed for digging. The mole's back paws are much smaller.

TEETH
Just behind the 11th ray of the star are incisor teeth. These act like tweezers, grabbing prey once that incredible nose has done its job.

NOSE
These odd moles are almost blind but at the end of their snout is a circle of 22 mobile tentacles, called rays, which helps them find food.

The star-nosed mole is more than just a skilled predator; it's a record-breaking one! That star-nose is actually the most sensitive sensory organ in the entire animal kingdom. Consisting of 11 pairs of finger-like tentacles, the star helps the mole to identify food. But that's not all. The mole's brain is able to process the information it receives from its nose at ultra high speeds. The mole can decide whether or not something is edible in about 25 milliseconds! Insects, small amphibians, and fish are all on the menu; thanks to that star-nose they can all be caught and eaten literally in the blink of an eye.

ACTUAL SIZE

▷ BELIEVE IT OR NOT, the star-nosed mole is an excellent swimmer! These little guinea pig-sized mammals live in wetland areas and hunt for food on the bottom of rivers and ponds as well as underground. A circle of pink, fleshy tentacles surround the mole's snout. These help it to find prey as well as to sense its way around underground. For all animals it is important to find and catch food as quickly as possible, otherwise they waste valuable energy. The star-nosed mole is such a speedy hunter that it can eat prey that other animals wouldn't waste their time tracking down.

Where in the world?

The star-nosed mole lives in wet lowland areas of eastern Canada and northeastern parts of the USA. It lives in networks of underground tunnels, some of which may lead directly to its feeding areas.

Did you know?

● *Nature* magazine awarded the star-nosed mole the title of "fastest-eating mammal" on Earth.

● The mole's star-nose contains more than 25,000 tiny sensory receptors. These are known as Eimer's organs after the German zoologist, Theodor Eimer (1843–1898), who first described these incredible receptors in 1871.

● Other species of moles also have Eimer's organs, but none of them have as many as the star-nosed mole.

● This amazing nose also allows the mole to smell underwater; this is something that, until recently, scientists thought was impossible! The mole does this by exhaling air bubbles onto its prey then inhaling the bubbles back in so that scents are carried to its nose.

● In addition to its sensitive nose, this amazing animal also has excellent hearing.

PHOTOFILE: Star-nosed Mole

▷ **Members of the family**
Moles may look like rodents, but they belong to the scientific family *Talpidae,* which includes shrew moles, desmans, and shrew-like digging animals. Star-nosed moles are probably the most flexible members of the group in diet and behavior.

FACT

Most moles like damp soil, which is much easier to dig through than dry, loose earth. If the soil is too dry, then the moles simply dig a little deeper or move to another, more suitable location. They may even occasionally come "topside" to hunt. As tunneling burns up a lot of energy, moles need to eat massive amounts of food to stay fueled up—around 60–100 percent of their body weight every day!

△ **Scooping claws**
A pair of large front claws
helps the mole to tunnel
through the earth. These are
slightly curved and backward-
facing so that soil can be
quickly scooped behind the
mole's body as it digs.

▷ **Tunneling for food**
Like other species of mole, the star-nose
digs shallow tunnels that it uses to forage
for food. When underground, those
tentacles can be closed up to stop soil
and food entering the nose.

Siberian Tiger

Scientific Name: *Panthera tigris altaica*

FUR
Keeping warm is a major problem for the Siberian tiger. Long, thick fur and an extra layer of body fat keeps out the cold.

EYES
As they mostly hunt at night, tigers rely on sight and scent to track prey. The tiger's forward-facing eyes (which give them binocular vision) help it to judge distances accurately.

PAWS
The tiger's paws have soft pads for silent hunting and long, sharp claws. When not in use, each claw retracts into a protective sheath.

LEGS
The tiger's back legs are longer than its front legs. This is an adaptation for jumping. The front paws can twist inward to hold prey.

If any creature fits the popular idea of what a predator should look like, it is the Siberian tiger (*Panthera tigris altaica*). This beautiful animal is the biggest of all the big cats—up to 11ft (3.3m) from head to tail. Its most obvious features are its huge head and powerful jaws, built for grabbing prey, snapping necks, and crunching bones. Despite its size, this hunter is as fast and agile as any cat. It can run at speeds of up to 50mph (80km/h) over short distances, but its preferred hunting technique relies on stealth. Creeping through the undergrowth, the tiger waits for prey to come close before pouncing on its victim. It will eat any available food; it will even tackle brown and black bears when hunger hits!

ACTUAL SIZE

▷ IT IS NEVER EASY being a single mother, but the Siberian tiger has a harder time than most new mothers. Tigers can have to up to six cubs at a time, but usually only a few of the youngsters will survive to adulthood. Poachers as well as other predators are an ever-present danger so, before she heads off to hunt, the female carries her cubs to the safety of a hidden den. Once the cubs are older, the mother tiger will begin to take them hunting with her, teaching them the skills that they will need to survive on their own.

Where in the world?

Siberian tigers are found mainly in Siberia, around the Sikhote Alin Mountain region and in the southwestern Primorye Province. In the past, small populations were reported in northeastern China and northern Korea.

Did you know?

• There are six subspecies of tiger: Bengal, Indochinese, Malayan, Siberian, South China, and Sumatran. The Malayan subspecies was only identified in 2004.

• The smallest is the Sumatran tiger. This can be a third of the weight of its Siberian relative.

• The largest tigers are found in the north, the smallest in the south. This is an example of Bergmann's Rule, which says that warm-blooded animals tend to increase in body size with increasing latitude and decreasing temperature.

• These beautiful cats are now very rare. It is estimated that fewer than 400 Siberian tigers survive in the wild.

• Powerful legs and a flexible backbone allow the tiger to cover distances of up to 33ft (10m) in a single bound.

PHOTOFILE: Siberian Tiger

▷ **Tiger teeth**
Sharp teeth and powerful jaws are used to kill and eat prey. The canines are especially large—up to 4in (10cm) long. Tiny barbs on the cat's tongue help it to scrape flesh from bone.

FACT
Siberia covers around 75 percent of Russia. Much of this region is "tundra"—a treeless upland where the ground stays frozen for many months. In these cold regions, the tigers need around 20lb (9kg) of meat a day to provide their bodies with enough fuel to stay warm. It is believed that all the world's tiger subspecies are descended from the Siberian tiger, which spread out across Europe and Asia during the Ice Age.

△ Larger males
Tigers are sexually dimorphic, meaning that males and females look different. Generally, males are around 30 percent bigger and heavier than females. Males also grow a prominent ruff of hair around their face.

▷ Snowshoe feet
The tiger's feet are large and wide. This helps to spread the cat's weight and stops it sinking into the snow. The front paws have five claws; the back paws have four.

American Mink

Scientific Name: *Neovison vison*

BACK PAWS
Mink spend much of their time in or around water. They have short legs and partial webbing on their back feet that makes them superb swimmers.

CARNASSIAL TEETH
Smaller, sharp teeth behind the canines are called carnassials. These work like a pair of scissors to slice a prey's flesh from the bone.

CANINE TEETH
Two pairs of long, dagger-like canine teeth (top and bottom) sit at the front of the mouth. These are used for grasping and killing prey.

Pound for pound, the American mink (*Neovison vison*) is one of the most powerful predators in the world. Like all members of the *Mustelidae* family, this small mammal is fast and feisty in a fight! Although it rarely grows bigger than 20in (51cm), the strength of its bite relative to its size is rivaled only by the Tasmanian devil and the American weasel. Mink climb and run well but it is in the water that this furry little predator is most at home. Anything from birds to muskrats are on the menu, but, with its partially webbed paws and streamlined body, the mink is primarily an aquatic hunter. It can dive to depths of 18ft (5.5m) in pursuit of prey such as fish and crustaceans.

ACTUAL SIZE

▷ THE MINK'S BEAUTIFULLY soft coat was almost the cause of this mammal's downfall. For centuries, wild mink have been hunted for their fur. At one point, their numbers fell so low that it became necessary to breed them on farms. Over the years, wild mink have either escaped or been released by animal rights groups. This has caused problems for other species, especially the European mink, which cannot compete with its more aggressive cousin. Attempts have been made to trap and kill these intruders. Not all traps are humane; many leave the animals injured.

Where in the world?

For the American mink, the ideal home is beside a slow-running stream, hidden by thick vegetation. They are naturally found throughout North America as far north as Alaska, although they tend to avoid desert regions.

Did you know?

● A popular legend, which comes from the Innu people of eastern Canada, describes the mink as "Earth-Divers" who dove to the ocean floor to bring up land for humans to live on.

● American mink are a speedy species. On land, they move with a bounding gait (the way an animal or person walks) and can reach speeds of up to 4mph (6.4km/h).

● The mink's hearing is tuned in to detect the high ultrasonic squeaks that rodents make.

● In one study, mink were tested to compare their intelligence with cats, ferrets, and skunks. The experiments were designed to see how well each animal could remember specific shapes, and the mink consistently came top of the class. They even performed better than primates in some tests!

PHOTOFILE: American Mink

▷ **Happy on land**
Mink are equally happy on land or in the water. They are good swimmers and skillful climbers. In fact, if they are alarmed, they will often run for cover to a riverside den or climb the nearest tree.

FACT
Many animals scent-mark their territory, leaving smelly messages at specific locations to warn off rivals or attract mates. Mustelids like skunks are famously smelly, but, according to the American zoologist Clinton Merriam (1855–1942), nothing matches the stench produced by a mink. Writing in 1886 he described it as: "one of the few substances, of animal, vegetable, or mineral origin, that has ... rendered me aware of the existence of the abominable sensation called nausea."

△ Mink shelters
American mink can dig their
own dens, but they usually take
over an abandoned burrow
from some other riverside
resident, like the muskrat.
They also use natural shelters
such as rock crevices.

▷ Traveling between dens
Male mink spend their time traveling
between one temporary den to the next,
taking several weeks to make a slow circuit
of their territory. In comparison, females
often use a single den all year round.

Spotted Hyena

Scientific Name: *Crocuta crocuta*

MANE
A short, erect mane on the neck and shoulders always stands upright. This makes the hyena look bigger and more dangerous to any potential predators.

HUNCH
The hyena's front legs are longer than its back legs, giving it a hunched look. Having a lower rear end makes it harder for attackers to grab hold.

JAWS
Large jaw muscles are attached to a sagittal crest. This is a ridge of bone running lengthwise along the middle of the top of the skull.

PAWS & CLAWS
Each foot has four toes. These are armed with short, stout claws. The claws are non-retractable, meaning that they can't be drawn back into the paw.

Most people think that hyenas are just scavengers. Although it is true that they will happily chase jackals and even lions away from a fresh kill, the spotted hyena (*Crocuta crocuta*) is also one of Africa's most proficient predators. That thick, muscular neck and powerful jaws gives the hyena the strongest bite of any mammal. It is fast too, with enough stamina to chase down prey over long distances while keeping up a pace of 37mph (60km/h). A lone hyena will hunt anything

ACTUAL SIZE

from rabbits to puff adders, but a hyena "clan" is almost unstoppable! Large clans work together to capture prey; such teamwork allows them to tackle animals as tough as a baby rhino or as fast as a gazelle.

▷ THE MORE HYENAS there are in the clan, the bigger the prey they can tackle. While hunting, the clan works together, rushing a herd to single out weak or sick individuals. A bite to the leg is enough to bring prey to its knees. The hyena's large front paws are perfect for pinning down their still-living victims as they tear off hunks of meat. Once a kill has been made, strict rules apply. Hyena clans are matriarchal and led by a dominant female. So females always eat first, followed by males, then cubs. Leftovers are carried off and buried to eat later.

Where in the world?

Spotted hyenas are found in sub-Saharan Africa, except in some parts of western and South Africa. They enjoy a surprisingly large range of habitats from the open grassland of the Serengeti to the Namib Desert.

Did you know?

● In terms of sheer bone-crushing power, the spotted hyena's jaws are stronger than those of a brown bear. This allows hyenas to eat practically every part of an animal, including bones, hooves, and teeth. A clan can consume a whole zebra in around half an hour!

● Hyenas are built for endurance. They have a massive heart, which accounts for 1 percent of their body weight (a lion's heart makes up 0.5 percent). This gives them incredible stamina when chasing down prey.

● Hyenas communicate using a wide variety of calls including a choked giggle, which has earned them the nickname "laughing hyenas."

● In problem-solving tests, hyenas outperform chimpanzees. They are even able to show their clan-mates how to solve the same problems. Chimps couldn't do that without training.

PHOTOFILE: Spotted Hyena

▷ **Vultures show the way**
Spotted hyenas use both sight and scent to track and kill their prey. However, they have also learned a valuable survival lesson: that the presence of vultures means there is a fresh kill close by.

FACT

Although spotted hyenas are widely regarded as scavengers that live off other animal's leftovers, studies have shown that they kill around 95 percent of all the food they eat. They are much more flexible predators than most of the big cats that they compete for food with. They can also adapt their diet and hunting techniques to take advantage of whatever the environment offers. They have even been known to hunt and kill lions!

△ **Living in clans**
Spotted hyenas have a
complex social life. Although
they live in large clans, the
group regularly splits into smaller
coalitions to hunt. Some individual
hyenas may even leave the clan to
go solo for a while.

▷ **Defending the territory**
To defend their territory, clan members use
a combination of scent marking and regular
boundary patrols. Long, "whooping" calls
are used to rally clan members to sites where
boundary conflicts might occur.

Platypus

Scientific Name: *Ornithorhynchus anatinus*

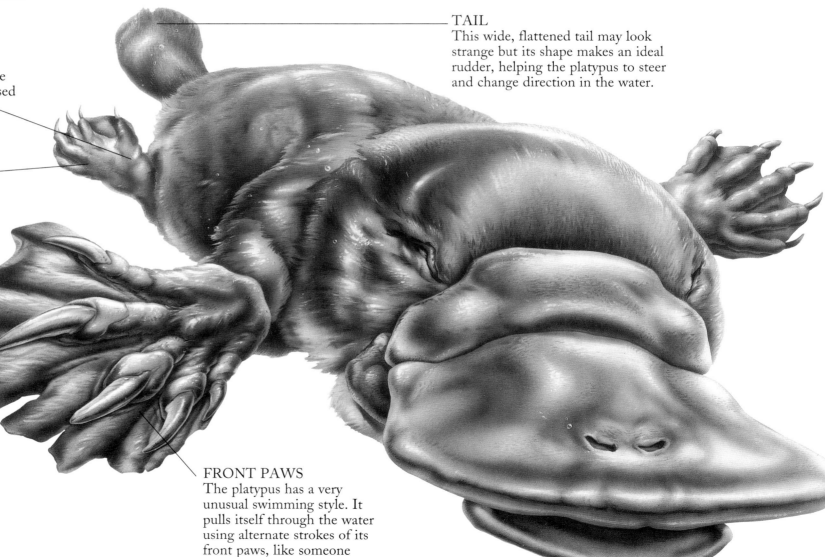

ANKLE SPUR
A spur on the back of the male's hind leg looks a little like a rose thorn. This is used to deliver a potent poison.

BACK PAWS
Although all four of the platypus' feet are partially webbed, only its front paws are used for swimming. The back feet and tail do the steering.

TAIL
This wide, flattened tail may look strange but its shape makes an ideal rudder, helping the platypus to steer and change direction in the water.

FRONT PAWS
The platypus has a very unusual swimming style. It pulls itself through the water using alternate strokes of its front paws, like someone rowing a boat.

With a beaver-like body, flat tail, and a "duckbill," the platypus (*Ornithorhynchus anatinus*) is a strange sight, but its odd attributes make it a skillful predator. Its streamlined body, powerful legs, and partially webbed feet power it through the water with minimum effort. Its fur is thick and waterproof, allowing it to stay warm even in cold mountain streams. It also has two adaptations that set it apart from most other mammals. The first is a spur on the ankle connected to a poison sac, making the platypus one of the few venomous mammals. The second is the sensitive bill, which can detect changes in pressure and the minute electric fields generated by living bodies.

ACTUAL SIZE

▷ THE PLATYPUS FEEDS on worms, insects, and crustaceans. To stay fit and healthy, it needs to eat about 20 percent of its body weight every day. Luckily it has the perfect tool for the job. As it dives into the water, the platypus shuts its eyes and ears, relying entirely on its bill to detect prey. This bill is really a sense organ, covered in special receptors that pick up the electric fields generated by muscle contractions. These are so accurate that they can detect prey up to 4in (10cm) away even if it is hidden under the mud.

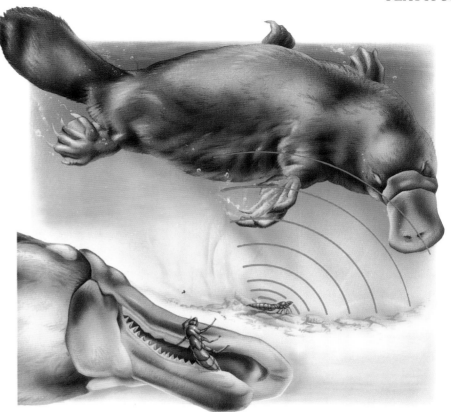

Where in the world?

These strange animals are one of Australia's most famous inhabitants. They are found in eastern Australia and Tasmania, ranging from cold, mountainous regions to tropical rainforests. They dig burrows in low-lying riverbanks, hidden by overhanging vegetation.

Did you know?

● When the first European scientists saw a platypus pelt in 1798 they thought that the skin was a fake made up from bits and pieces of other animals. The Scottish anatomist Robert Knox (1791–1862) even described it as a "freak imposture."

● Platypus venom is made up of a cocktail of more than 20 different chemicals. The venom is used more for defense rather than attack, although it is powerful enough to kill or temporarily paralyze small animals.

● The platypus lays eggs, like a reptile, instead of giving birth to live young like other mammals. However, the word mammal comes from "mammary glands." Although the platypus lays eggs, it still feeds its young on milk produced by mammary glands. Therefore the platypus is a mammal and not a reptile.

PHOTOFILE: Platypus

▷ **Platypus bill**
The platypus is born with teeth, which drop out at an early age. Fossilized remains show that the adult platypus originally had teeth too, but, as the bill evolved into a specialized feeding tool, teeth became less useful.

FACT

In 1998, a ten-year-long search along the southern coastline of Victoria, Australia, uncovered the oldest platypus fossils ever found. The discovery led scientists to conclude that the platypus species may be up to 120 million years old, meaning that it lived alongside the dinosaurs. There were many kinds of mammals living in the age of the dinosaurs, but none, apart from the platypus family, is still alive today.

△ Water hunter
Although it hunts in the water, the platypus spends up to 17 hours a day resting out of the water in an underground burrow. Two types of burrows are used: nesting burrows and camping burrows.

▷ Food storage
The platypus uses its broad tail as a fat reserve for when food is in short supply. The Tasmanian devil, the fat-tailed sheep, and the fat-tailed gecko all have a similar adaptation.

Gray Wolf

Scientific Name: *Canis lupus*

BODY
A well-fed wolf has a layer of fat beneath its skin. This reserve helps it to survive when food is scarce in the winter months.

FEMALE & MALE
Female wolves are smaller then the males. They have less muscle bulk around the shoulders, a narrower head and muzzle, and slightly shorter legs.

FUR
Long, thick winter fur helps keep the wolf warm. In warmer weather, the fur is shorter and thinner. Coat color ranges from almost white to black.

LEGS
The gray wolf has slightly longer legs than other wolf species. This allows it to cope better with the deep snow that covers most of its habitat.

Wolves have been our companions ever since prehistoric times. Those wolves that visited human settlements for food eventually evolved into our best friend: the dog. Those that kept their distance remained our enemies. Luckily, despite our attempts to wipe out the gray wolf (*Canis lupus*) they still survive in the world's wild spaces. This adaptable animal will eat almost anything. Smaller prey is killed quickly with a bite to the neck. The wolf doesn't have the physical bulk to take on big prey alone, but it doesn't need to as it can hunt in a pack. Wolves work together to make a big kill, chasing, biting, and clawing an animal until it drops from blood loss and exhaustion.

ACTUAL SIZE

▷ A WOLF HUNT is like a well-organized military campaign—these wolves know exactly what is expected of them at every stage of the battle. Stage One: Locating Prey. Wolves use their powerful sense of smell to catch wind of prey. Stage Two: Stalking Prey. The pack tries to get as close as they can before they attack. Stage Three: The Encounter. The pack surround their prey. This moose may be outnumbered, but it's not about to give up easily! Stage Four: The Chase. The moose runs for its life. The wolves give chase hoping to eventually exhaust their prey.

Where in the world?

Hunting and loss of habitat has driven the gray wolf out of all but the world's most secluded regions. These magnificent hunters are now found only in remote areas of northern Asia, Europe, and North America.

Did you know?

• In Norse myth it was believed that, at the end of the world (Ragnarök), the children of the giant wolf Fenris would devour the Sun and the Moon.

• Wolves live in tightly knit family packs. Mother and father (called the alpha dogs) do the bulk of the work during a hunt and always eat first after a kill.

• In some areas, gray wolves compete with black bears for food and will kill them if they get the chance.

• When chasing prey, a gray wolf can reach speeds up 43mph (69km/h) for short periods.

• Although a pack is useful when hunting large prey animals, the first wolf reintroduced to Sweden after the species had been wiped out regularly killed moose on its own.

PHOTOFILE: Gray Wolf

▷ **Wolf pups**
The average wolf litter is five to six pups. Pups are usually born in the spring when prey is plentiful. At birth, they are blind, deaf, and covered in soft gray fur.

FACT

Hunting is not always successful, so a wolf's body is designed for feast or famine. When food is plentiful the wolf will gorge itself, and it can eat almost 20 percent of its body weight in a single sitting. A healthy wolf will always have some excess body fat. This acts as a reserve when prey is scarce. They can live on this reserve for up to 14 days with no permanent ill-effects.

△ **Howling wolf**
Do wolves howl at the moon?
Although wolves certainly howl
as a way of staying in touch
with their pack-mates over long
distances, there is no evidence that
the moon inspires any particular
form of communication.

▷ **Water lovers**
Wolves love water. They play in it, use
it to cool themselves, and even swim for
fun. They also need to drink fresh water
regularly, unlike some predators who get
water from the bodies of their prey.

Anteater

Scientific Name: *Myrmecophaga tridactyla*

FUR
The anteater's body is covered with stiff, straw-like hair. This is especially long on the tail, making the animal look larger than it actually is.

SNOUT & MOUTH
The giant anteater's tube-like "snout" is really an elongated jaw. At its tip is a small black nose and a tiny mouth opening.

FRONT CLAWS
Front claws grow up to 4in (10cm) long. These claws are curved, which makes it easier for the anteater to break open termite mounds.

PAWS
Like African apes, the giant anteater walks on its front knuckles. This stops its long, curved, front claws from being blunted as it walks.

The giant anteater (*Myrmecophaga tridactyla*) is a peculiar predator. It's easy to imagine that this muscular animal preys on other mammals, but it actually lives on ants and termites. If we look at that odd body, we can see how well it's suited to the task. The anteater has powerful limbs and sharp claws to tear open anthills and termite mounds. It doesn't have teeth, but that tube-like snout and long, sticky tongue can lap up around 35,000 ants and termites a day. According to the American biologist E.O. Wilson, there are between one and ten quadrillion ants in the world! It makes good sense to take advantage of such a plentiful food source, and the giant anteater is perfectly adapted to do so.

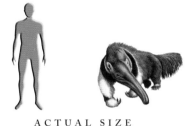

ACTUAL SIZE

▷ THIS ANT NEST LOOKS like a tasty treat and well worth making that extra effort for. Using its tail like a prop, the hungry anteater rears up on its powerful back legs. Its sharp claws make short work of the tough mud walls of the ant nest, but the anteater has to eat quickly. Soon, soldier ants will come swarming out to attack, biting and spraying formic acid on the intruder. Luckily, the anteater can flick its tongue in and out up to 160 times per minute. At this speed, it takes only a few minutes until it has eaten its fill.

Where in the world?

Giant anteaters are natives of central and South America. The species is found all the way from Honduras to northern Argentina, where it lives in both tropical rainforests and on the drier grass and shrublands.

Did you know?

• Ants are not an especially energy-rich food source, so to save energy the anteater sleeps for around ten hours day.

• *Myrmecophaga tridactyla* is Greek for "three-fingered anteater." Despite this, the anteater actually has five toes on each foot.

• Female anteaters give birth to just one baby at a time. These young anteaters (called pups) can sometimes be seen riding on their mother's back.

• The giant anteater's sense of smell is 40 times more sensitive than a human's.

• The giant anteater is more than capable of protecting itself from bigger predators. When trouble strikes, it rears up on its hind legs. Using its tail for balance, it lashes out with its huge front claws. Using this technique, it can even fight off big cats such as jaguars.

PHOTOFILE: Anteater

▷ **Fur as armor**
The anteater's long, thick fur doesn't just keep it warm and dry, although it is very good at that. It also acts like armor, protecting the anteater from stings and bites from the insects that it eats.

FACT

Although some anteaters are no bigger than a squirrel, the giant anteater really lives up to its name, growing up to 7ft (2.1m) from the tip of its snout to the end its tail. This massive creature is a member of the order *Pilosa*, which also includes sloths. Within this group, the giant anteater is the most terrestrial species, spending most of its time on the ground rather than in the treetops.

△ Sticky tongue
At the very end of the giant anteater's jaw is a tiny mouth. Inside is a long, thin, sticky tongue that measures up to 24in (61cm) long. This is used to lap up ants.

▷ Eating without teeth
Before food can be digested, it needs to be broken down. The anteater doesn't have teeth and can't chew so its food is crushed against the hard palate at the top of the tube-like mouth.

Ghost Bat

Scientific Name: *Macroderma gigas*

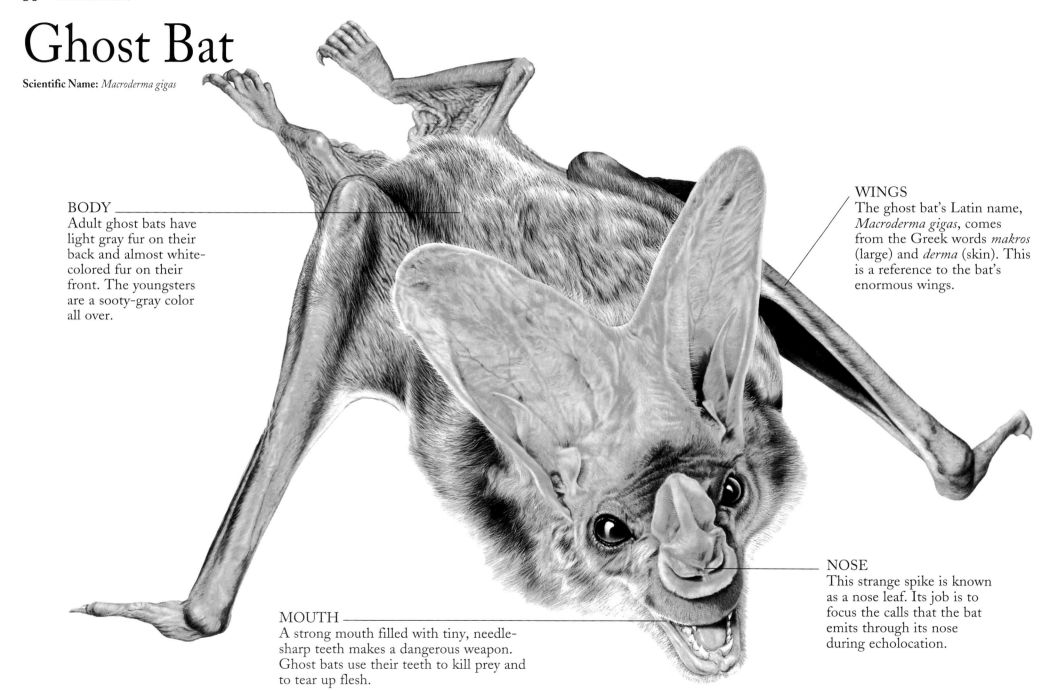

BODY
Adult ghost bats have light gray fur on their back and almost white-colored fur on their front. The youngsters are a sooty-gray color all over.

WINGS
The ghost bat's Latin name, *Macroderma gigas*, comes from the Greek words *makros* (large) and *derma* (skin). This is a reference to the bat's enormous wings.

NOSE
This strange spike is known as a nose leaf. Its job is to focus the calls that the bat emits through its nose during echolocation.

MOUTH
A strong mouth filled with tiny, needle-sharp teeth makes a dangerous weapon. Ghost bats use their teeth to kill prey and to tear up flesh.

Other bats may be content to feed on fruit or the occasional insect, but this large flying mammal has an appetite to match its size. The ghost bat (*Macroderma gigas*) is Australia's only meat-eating bat. It feeds on anything from other bats to small birds. It is a skilled flyer and is easily able to catch prey in the air. It will also attack animals on the ground, dropping on its victims from above, wrapping them in its fleshy wings and killing them with a bite to the head or neck. Once a kill has been made, nothing goes to waste. Ghost bats are superbly efficient eaters. Bones, fur, and feathers are all consumed along with their victim's flesh, which is sliced up by rows of needle-sharp teeth.

ACTUAL SIZE

▷ LEAVING THE ROOST shortly after sunset, the ghost bat uses a combination of superb hearing and echolocation to home in on a meal. Mice, bats, birds, lizards, and snakes are the bat's preferred prey, but when food is scarce even an insect, like this moth, makes a tasty treat. Finding a handy place to roost, the bat eats its meal, whole, before flying off to find more food. Unless it can find bigger prey, it will be many more hours before it can head back to the safety of its cave, where it rests up during the daylight hours.

Where in the world?

The ghost bat is local to Australia. This means that it is found nowhere else. At present these large bats are found in northern Australia, western Australia, Queensland, and the Northern Territory, but they are becoming increasingly rare.

Did you know?

• Mammals such as flying foxes, squirrels, and lemurs can all glide using a flap of skin stretched between the wrist and ankle, like a parachute. However, bats are the only mammals that are capable of sustained and controlled flight, like birds.

• Young ghost bats begin flying when they are only seven weeks old. At three months old they are ready to start eating meat!

• Ghost bats kill small prey with a bite to the head or the back of the neck, just like the vampires of legend. This has led to them being nicknamed "false vampire bats."

• Other species of false vampire bat (*Megadermatidae* Family) are found in central Africa and southern Asia. The Australian species, *Macroderma gigas*, is the largest member of the family. In fact, *gigas* means "giant."

PHOTOFILE: Ghost Bat

▷ **White as a ghost**
The ghost bat gets its common name from its ghostly white appearance and its ability to fly almost silently. Its white fur makes it one of the easiest members of the bat family to identify.

FACT

For a human to hang upside down like a bat would take a lot of energy. It requires a lot of muscle power to get a good grip and hold on to a surface. Bat biology, however, has adapted to an upside-down existence. So to hold onto a surface, the bat actually relaxes rather than tense its muscles! This means that bats can literally hang around all day without expending any energy.

△ **Safety upside down**
Bats roost hanging upside down for a number of reasons, but safety is an important factor. Because they can hang almost anywhere, they can take advantage of hidden roosts such as ceilings or cave walls.

▷ **Glider power**
Bats also roost upside down because they don't have the wing power to take off from a dead start, like birds. So they climb to a high spot and then drop into a glide.

Leopard

Scientific Name: *Panthera pardus*

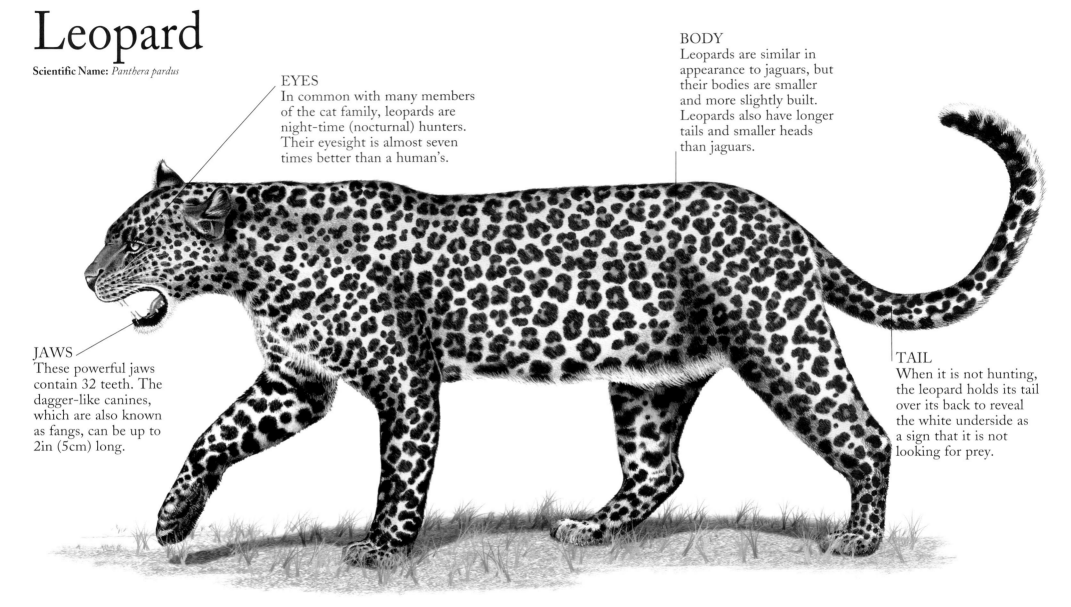

EYES
In common with many members of the cat family, leopards are night-time (nocturnal) hunters. Their eyesight is almost seven times better than a human's.

BODY
Leopards are similar in appearance to jaguars, but their bodies are smaller and more slightly built. Leopards also have longer tails and smaller heads than jaguars.

JAWS
These powerful jaws contain 32 teeth. The dagger-like canines, which are also known as fangs, can be up to 2in (5cm) long.

TAIL
When it is not hunting, the leopard holds its tail over its back to reveal the white underside as a sign that it is not looking for prey.

Graceful and agile, the leopard (*Panthera pardus*) is perhaps the most athletic member of the cat family. These remarkable beasts are equally skilled at running, jumping, climbing, and swimming. But when it comes to hunting, leopards are natural-born killers that feed on around 92 different species. Stalking almost silently through the undergrowth, the leopard uses both surprise and speed to make a kill. These cool cats can jump more than 15ft (4.6m) and once they have their paws, claws, and jaws on their prey, there's no escape. That athletic body is strong, too. A fully grown leopard can haul three times its own body weight up a 20ft (6m) tree, where it can enjoy its meal undisturbed.

ACTUAL SIZE

▷ UNLIKE LIONS, LEOPARDS are solitary creatures. Mother leopards raise their cubs on their own, without a pack or partner to help. So this new mom needs all her stealth and intelligence. Female leopards may have up to four cubs at a time. The female keeps them well hidden in her den while she goes out hunting. For the first three months, cubs feed on mother's milk. Later, she will share her kill with the cubs. It's only when she has taught them how to hunt that cubs will catch food for themselves, although the family may stay together for up to two years.

Where in the world?

Leopards are one of the most widespread species of big cat. They are found in eastern and central Africa. Scattered populations also exist in southern and central Asia, in the Indian subcontinent, and in China.

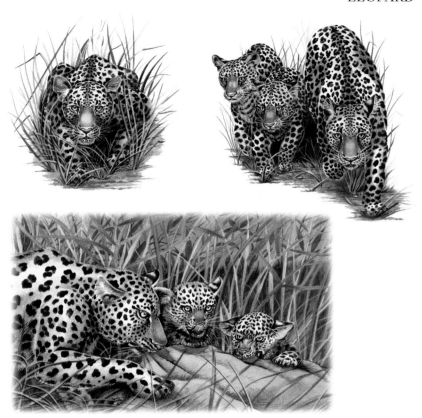

Did you know?

• Black panthers are not a separate species of big cat. They are simply jaguars, leopards, or tigers with all-black coats. White panthers and even pinkish "strawberry" leopards also exist.

• It wasn't until 1758 that leopards were classified as a species. It used to be believed that leopards were a cross between a lion and a tiger. A real cross between a lion and a tiger is known as a liger or a tiglon. Such crosses do not occur naturally, as the species live in different parts of the world.

• "Rogue" leopards have been known to hunt humans for food, although it is very rare. The panar leopard, for example, killed more than 400 people after it was injured by a hunter and left unable to catch its usual prey.

PHOTOFILE: Leopard

▷ **Rosette markings**
Leopards and cheetahs are easily confused as both of these big cats have distinctive orange-spotted fur. However, cheetahs have simple black spots, evenly spread over their bodies. Leopards have rounder, smaller "rosettes."

FACT
Leopards are opportunistic and adaptable predators that will eat almost anything that they have the chance to kill! Their diet ranges from dung beetles to crocodiles, depending on their environment and the availability of prey. On open grasslands they are most likely to hunt hoofed, grass-eating "ungulates." In Africa this includes antelopes and gazelles; in India, muntjac deer are their preferred prey. In forested regions leopards will hunt monkeys or other tree-dwelling mammals.

△ **Killer's teeth**
Sharp-edged carnassial teeth along the sides of the leopard's jaws are used to slice meat from the bone. Small incisors rip off the prey's fur, while the large incisors (or fangs) deliver the killing bite.

▷ **All in the family**
There are at least nine known subspecies of leopard: African, Amur, Arabian, Indian, Indochinese, Javan, North Chinese, Persian, and Sri Lankan. These look superficially similar but vary in size and weight.

Pyrenean Desman

Scientific Name: *Galemys pyrenaicus*

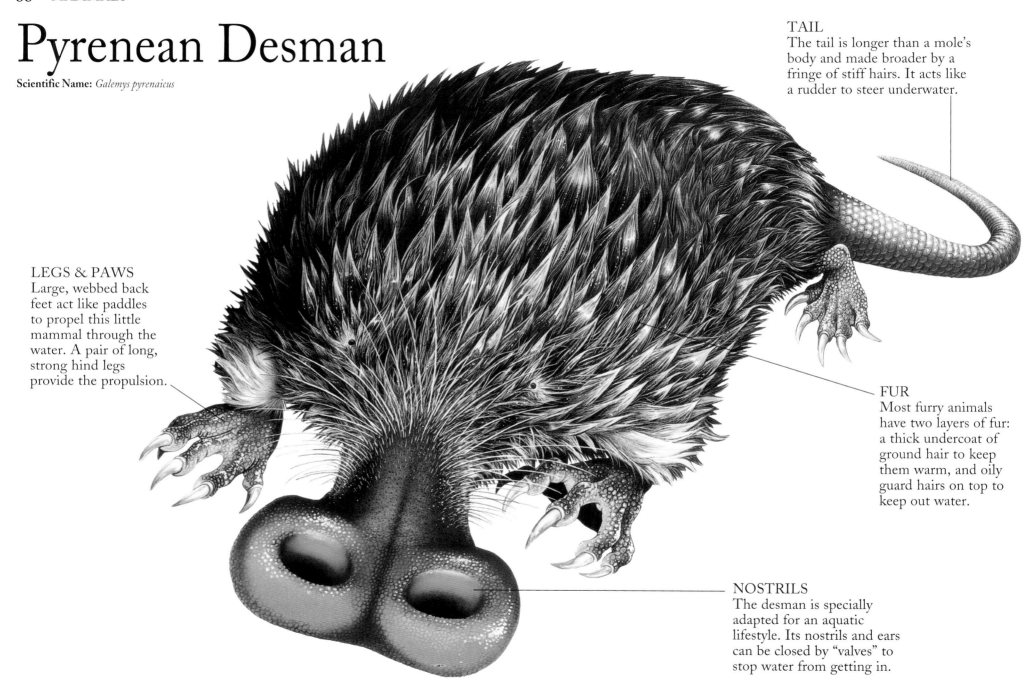

TAIL
The tail is longer than a mole's body and made broader by a fringe of stiff hairs. It acts like a rudder to steer underwater.

LEGS & PAWS
Large, webbed back feet act like paddles to propel this little mammal through the water. A pair of long, strong hind legs provide the propulsion.

FUR
Most furry animals have two layers of fur: a thick undercoat of ground hair to keep them warm, and oily guard hairs on top to keep out water.

NOSTRILS
The desman is specially adapted for an aquatic lifestyle. Its nostrils and ears can be closed by "valves" to stop water from getting in.

Could anything be stranger than the Pyrenean desman (*Galemys pyrenaicus*)? This creature is closely related to the mole, but unlike its cousin, spends most of its life in the water. This semi-aquatic hunter preys on insects, amphibians, small fish, and crustaceans such as shrimp and snails. It is well adapted to its watery habitat, with a streamlined body, long rudder-like tail, and powerful webbed hind feet. What makes the desman such an expert predator is that strange nose.

ACTUAL SIZE

It is extremely long, flexible, and sensitive. The desman has poor eyesight, but using its nose to "feel" for prey, it can catch up to a third of its body weight every day while hunting in almost total darkness.

▷ SIFTING THROUGH SEDIMENT with its forefeet, the desman is on the hunt. Down at the bottom of the river there's not much to see, but that long snout works just as well as a pair of eyes. This amazing nose is around 1in (2.5cm) long—that's about a fifth of the desman's body length. Unlike the rest of its body, the snout isn't furry. Instead, it is covered in rows of whisker-like hairs called vibrissae. These can detect the smallest movements, allowing the desman to hone in on nearby prey. That is bad news for this stonefly, but good news for this hungry hunter.

Where in the world?

Pyrenean desmans take their name from the Pyrenees Mountains, dividing Spain and France, where they are traditionally found. They prefer fast-flowing rivers and mountain streams, but are occasionally found in canals, lakes, and marshes.

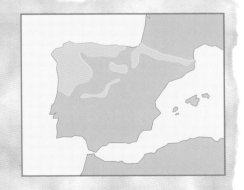

Did you know?

• Some scientists believe that desmans may use echolocation to help hunt for prey. It has been suggested that desmans slap the water with their tail and use their sensitive snout to "feel" for echoes, thereby building up a mental image of their surroundings.

• The shape of the desman's nose has earned it the nickname of trumpet rat.

• While Russian desmans are sociable animals, its Pyrenean relative is very aggressive toward other members of its own species. In the breeding season it will happily share its den with a mate, but it has been known to fight to the death with intruders.

• Desmans were once hunted for their sleek, thick fur. Although they are now protected by law, destruction of their habitat threatens the continued survival of both species.

PHOTOFILE: Pyrenean Desman

▷ **Snout explorer**
Like an elephant's trunk, the desman's snout is used to help this curious creature to explore its environment. It is not only a very sensitive tool for touching and identifying objects, but is also flexible and moveable.

FACT

Desmans are a group of ancient animals whose roots can be traced back millions of years. Today, however, just two species remain: the little Pyrenean desman and its Russian relative, *Desmana moschata*, which is larger and furrier than its Spanish cousin. Both the Russian and Pyrenean species are thought to be very sensitive to water pollution. Scientists are currently studying both species to learn more about what they need to thrive and survive.

△ Borrowing shelters
Desmans like to live close to water where the hunting is good. However, they don't usually dig their own shelters. Instead, they use abandoned water rat burrows or take cover in ready-made rock crevices.

▷ Adapted for swimming
Pyrenean desmans are also called desman moles. However, while moles have powerful back legs for digging, desmans have powerful back legs for swimming. The front legs are kept tucked away, giving a streamlined shape underwater.

Leopard Seal

Scientific Name: *Hydrurga leptonyx*

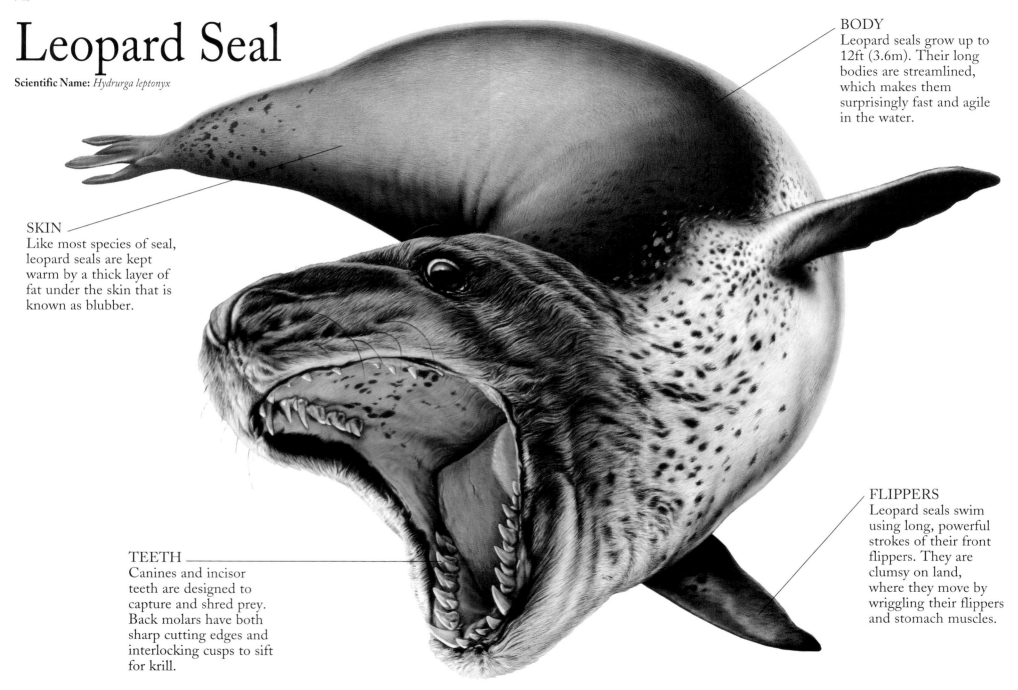

BODY
Leopard seals grow up to 12ft (3.6m). Their long bodies are streamlined, which makes them surprisingly fast and agile in the water.

SKIN
Like most species of seal, leopard seals are kept warm by a thick layer of fat under the skin that is known as blubber.

TEETH
Canines and incisor teeth are designed to capture and shred prey. Back molars have both sharp cutting edges and interlocking cusps to sift for krill.

FLIPPERS
Leopard seals swim using long, powerful strokes of their front flippers. They are clumsy on land, where they move by wriggling their flippers and stomach muscles.

The leopard seal (*Hydrurga leptonyx*) is sometimes called the sea leopard—and for a very good reason. This aquatic hunter is one of Antarctica's top predators, second only to the killer whale. Most seals enjoy a diet of fish and crustaceans, but the leopard seal also has a taste for warm-blooded prey. It regularly hunts other species of seal, but penguins are its favorite food. Lying in wait for newly fledged penguins to enter the water, the leopard seal is a patient predator. When it strikes, it moves with amazing agility for a creature that weighs in at more than 1,000lb (450kg). Holding its prey in its huge mouth, it shakes it like a rag doll, shredding the victim into bite-sized chunks.

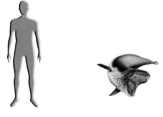

ACTUAL SIZE

▷ IN 1985, THE SCOTTISH explorer Gareth Wood was bitten twice on the leg when a leopard seal surged out of the water beside him and tried to drag him down into the ocean. His companions only managed to save him by kicking the animal in the head with their spiked boots. Eventually the seal backed off and returned to the water, allowing Gareth to be carried back to the safety of base. Although attacks on humans by leopard seals are very rare, Antarctic explorers are warned about the dangers of getting too close to these dangerous, and potentially deadly, predators.

Where in the world?

Leopard seals are found along the coast of Antarctica and around most sub-Antarctic islands, especially where penguins breed. Some venture as far north as South America and New Zealand in search of food.

Did you know?

● The explorer Ernest Shackleton (1874–1922) recorded that during his 1914–16 Antarctic expedition, a member of his team (Thomas Orde-Lees) was skiing across sea ice when a leopard seal emerged from between two ice floes and gave chase. The seal eventually dived into an open lane of water and, following Orde-Lees' shadow, emerged on the ice in front of his "prey." He was only saved when Frank Wild, Shackleton's second-in-command, shot the seal dead.

● In 1999, inflatable boats at the U.S. Antarctic base Palmer were fitted with puncture guards after being repeatedly attacked and sunk by leopard seals.

● They may be clumsy on land, but in their natural element leopard seals can swim at speeds of up to 25mph (40km/h).

PHOTOFILE: Leopard Seal

▷ **What's in a name**
The leopard seal's scientific name comes from two Greek words. *Hydrurga* means "water worker" and *leptonyx* means "small clawed." The species was first identified by the French zoologist Henri Marie Ducrotay de Blainville (1777–1850) in 1830.

FACT

Like most aquatic animals, leopard seal bodies are well adapted for an underwater life. Seals don't have gills, so they cannot absorb oxygen from the water, like fish. However, they can store three times as much oxygen in their blood and muscles as a human of the same weight. This means that they are able to stay submerged for at least 10 minutes. Other species of seal can stay underwater for up to an hour!

△ Diving underwater
When it dives, the seal's
nostrils automatically shut
to keep out the water. As it
opens its mouth to catch prey,
its tongue and the soft palate
move up to stop water from
entering the lungs.

▷ Battle of the bulls
Male leopard seals (bulls) fight to win
the right to mate with the females. Such
battles can be bloody affairs as they
bludgeon one another and attempt to sink
their teeth into their opponent's neck.

Solenodon

Scientific Name:: *Solenodon cubanus & Solenodon paradoxus*

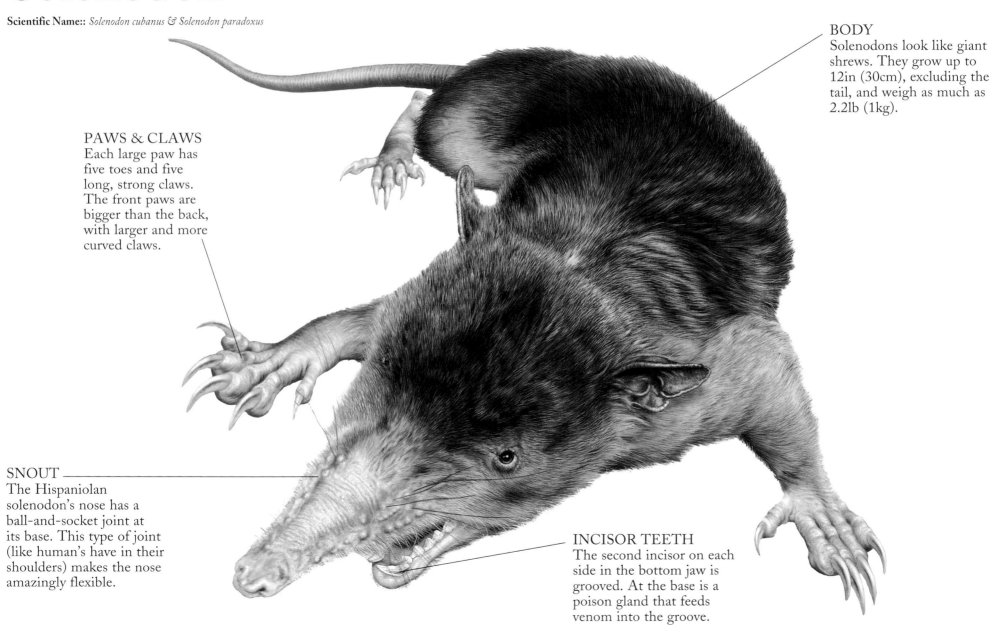

BODY
Solenodons look like giant shrews. They grow up to 12in (30cm), excluding the tail, and weigh as much as 2.2lb (1kg).

PAWS & CLAWS
Each large paw has five toes and five long, strong claws. The front paws are bigger than the back, with larger and more curved claws.

SNOUT
The Hispaniolan solenodon's nose has a ball-and-socket joint at its base. This type of joint (like human's have in their shoulders) makes the nose amazingly flexible.

INCISOR TEETH
The second incisor on each side in the bottom jaw is grooved. At the base is a poison gland that feeds venom into the groove.

The solenodon is a little predator with a big problem. Before Europeans arrived on the islands of Hispaniola and Cuba, solenodon (*Solenodon cubanus*; also *Solenodon paradoxus*) were one of the dominant carnivores. These shrew-like mammals have massive claws for digging up prey such as termites and beetles. These claws give them a good enough grip to be able to climb near-vertical surfaces in search of tasty treats like reptiles. They have a poisonous bite, and are said to be able to kill prey as large as chickens. However, the solenodon is not equipped for modern living. The arrival of cats and rats on the previously isolated islands has devastated their numbers.

ACTUAL SIZE

▷ WHEN ANIMALS FIGHT, it is usually over territory or a mate. These fights are stylized affairs. The aim is to show that you are bigger and more powerful than your rival, not necessarily to kill it. In the wild, the animal facing defeat usually backs off, but it has been reported that solenodons always fight to the death. As solenodons are not immune to their own venom, deaths during such conflicts are possible. These observations need to be considered though. When captive animals fight, the loser has nowhere to retreat to, so the fight may last longer than in the wild.

Where in the world?

These rare mammals are only found on the islands Cuba and Hispaniola (which is shared between Haiti and the Dominican Republic). There are two distinct species: the Hispaniolan solenodon and the Cuban.

Did you know?

● The female solenodon's teats are located near the animal's backside.

● Apparently solenodons never run in a straight line. According to villagers who live close to solenodon habitats, these strange animals- always run on their toes in a zigzagging pattern.

● Solenodons have scent glands in their armpits and their groin. These are said to give off an odor that smells like a goat!

● At one time, both species of solenodon were believed to be extinct. Even today little is known about their lives or habits.

● The solenodon's vision is not great, but it has a superb sense of hearing, smell, and touch.

● The name solenodon comes from the Greek for "grooved tooth."

PHOTOFILE: Solenodon

▷ **Two Species**
The two known species of solenodon are easily distinguished from each another. The Hispaniolan species (shown in the photo on the right) has reddish-brownish fur, while its Cuban cousin has dark brown, almost black, fur.

FACT
These incredible creatures are descended from a species that first appeared on Earth around 30 million years ago! During that time the species has changed very little and they are now regarded as examples of "living fossils." The Cuban solenodon was thought to be extinct until March 2012. After a ten-year search, a team of researchers found a population in the mountainous Alejandro de Humboldt National Park, on the northeastern end of Cuba.

△ Sensitive nose
This incredibly flexible nose
allows the little hunter to search
for insects even in the smallest
of spaces. It allows the animal to
investigate narrow crevices where
potential prey may be hiding.

▷ Hiding underground
These peculiar-looking mammals are solitary
and shy creatures. They spend much of their
day hidden away in underground burrows.
Even when they do emerge at night time to
hunt, they are rarely seen.

Grizzly Bear

Scientific Name: *Ursus arctos horribilis*

BACK
This distinctive hump is where a mass of muscles is attached to the bear's backbone, giving the animal additional strength for digging and catching prey.

BODY
The grizzly bear can be distinguished from other species of bear by its size, the hump between its shoulders, and its long, curved claws.

FUR
These fabulous bears get their name from their color. Their fur is generally brown, tipped with white. This makes them look grizzled (streaked with gray).

CLAWS
Curved claws on the bear's front feet help with climbing, digging, picking fruit, and catching prey. Claws can be 4in (10cm) long.

The grizzly bear is a flexible eater, able to make the best of whatever Mother Nature has to offer. In the fall and spring, it grazes on fruit, nuts, and small mammals. As the weather warms up though, it turns its attention to something more substantial. The summer brings a haul of salmon upstream to spawn (lay eggs). Grizzlies are expert fishermen and one bear may catch a dozen salmon a day. However, fishing is just a sideline. This bear is the top predator in its range and animals including moose, elk, caribou, and deer are regularly on the menu. Those paws, claws, and jaws make a menacing combination and they can bring down most large mammals with a single blow.

ACTUAL SIZE

▷ "BEWARE OF BEARS" is a very real warning in some parts of the world. Grizzlies are not naturally aggressive toward humans, but when they have young cubs to protect, bear mothers will take on all comers—as this hiker has discovered. Running for his life, the hiker takes to the trees, but the grizzly manages to maul the intruder's leg before he can pull himself to safety. Losing his grip, the hiker falls to the ground, and into the waiting jaws of the angry grizzly. The only chance the hiker has now is to play dead and hope the bear loses interest.

Where in the world?

Grizzly bears once roamed throughout the western United States, Canada, and Mexico. Hunting and human habitation has drastically reduced their numbers. Today they are mainly found in Alaska, western Canada, and scattered northwestern states.

Did you know?

● Winter is a difficult time for most animals. The solution for many is hibernation. This is a sleep-like state during which the animal lowers its body temperature and heart rate to save energy. Zoologists aren't sure whether bears hibernate or simply become dormant in the winter. However, as they "sleep" they can burn up a million calories. So, by the spring, many bears have lost a third of their body weight.

● When the American naturalist George Ord (1781–1866) gave the grizzly its Latin name in 1815, he confused grizzly (meaning streaked with gray) with grisly, meaning horrible. That is why these bears carry the name *Ursus arctos horribilis*.

● These powerful bears can run at speeds of up to 35mph (56km/h).

PHOTOFILE: Grizzly Bear

▷ **It's a hard life**
Life in the wild, outdoors, can be tough. In captivity, a grizzly bear can expect to live as long as 47 years. In the wild, its life expectancy may fall as low as 15 years.

FACT

Grizzly bears are a subspecies of brown bear. These highly adaptable mammals live on grasslands, scrublands, and in mountainous, forested regions. Their size depends on the availability of food. Generally, Canadian bears have a richer and more varied diet, so tend to be bigger than the grizzlies found in the American Rocky Mountains. Some of the smallest grizzlies live in the Yukon, where adults can be half the size of bears in other regions.

△ **Height and weight**
Grizzly bears measure up to 4ft (1.2m) when standing on all fours and up to 8ft (2.4m) when standing upright. These bears can weigh 400–1,700lb (181–771kg).

▷ **Teeth for a varied diet**
The grizzly bear's teeth reflect its varied (omnivorous) diet. It has four large incisor teeth (or fangs) to tear flesh. However, their other teeth are not as sharp as those of strict carnivores.

Short-beaked Echidna

Scientific Name: *Tachyglossus aculeatus*

SPINES
Spines are the perfect defense against predators. When danger strikes, the echidna simply rolls itself into a ball. Fur between the spines provides insulation.

BEAK
Despite its name, the "beak" is actually quite long. Echidnas grow up to 18in (46cm) long, with a 3in (7.5cm) beak.

LEGS & CLAWS
Short, powerful legs and sharp claws help the echidna to dig. The claws on both of the echidna's front and back feet are long and are curved backward.

TONGUE
The tongue is the echidna's main means of catching prey. It can stick out up to 7in (18cm) outside of the animal's beak.

This spiky critter is an ant-eating machine! The echidna feeds by using its powerful forearms and claws to tear apart logs and dig open anthills and termite mounds. Once inside, the echidna laps up the contents with speedy flicks of its long, sticky tongue. The echidna's eyesight is quite poor, but that doesn't matter. It has excellent hearing and that long, tube-like beak is covered in sensitive receptors that react to heat, movement, and the weak electric fields generated by living bodies.

ACTUAL SIZE

The echidna will eat anything that it can suck up, including worms, but even big, armored termites are no problem. On the roof of that mouth are backward-facing "plates" that grind up tough termites with ease!

▷ THE ECHIDNA BELONGS to a very specialist group of animals known as monotremes. Unlike most mammals and marsupials, monotremes lay eggs rather than giving birth to live young. After the leathery egg has been laid, the female echidna puts it directly into her pouch. It takes around ten days to hatch and the young echidna (known as a puggle) will stay there feeding for a further 55 days. When the puggle starts to grow spines, the Mother moves her prickly lodger from her pouch to a burrow, where it stays until it is fully weaned. This can take around seven months.

Where in the world?

Echidnas are common throughout Australia, in Tasmania, and in lowland regions of New Guinea. They have been affected less by changes in land use than most Australian animals and thrive wherever ants and termites are plentiful.

Did you know?

● The echidna has a bigger brain than similar-sized animals.

● These spiny anteaters are named after Echidna the Mother of All Monsters, who, according to ancient Greek mythology, was a beautiful water nymph with the body of a hideous snake. This is a reference to the fact that the echidna, like the mythical monster, has the physical attributes of both mammals and reptiles (it lays eggs).

● The echidna is one of Australia's most popular animals. They have appeared on the country's stamps and coins. Millie the Echidna was a mascot for Sydney's Olympic Games in 2000.

● Echidnas swim to cool themselves down. When they do, they keep their beak above water, like a snorkel.

● The famous *Sonic the Hedgehog* video game featured a character called Knuckles the Echidna.

PHOTOFILE: Short-beaked Echidna

▷ **Changing names**
Since the species was discovered in 1792, echidnas have had four name changes. Its modern name, *Tachyglossus aculeatus*, means "spiny quick tongue." Echidnas are sometimes called spiny anteaters, although they are no relation to South American anteaters.

FACT

All animals groom themselves to keep their fur clean, waterproof, and free from lice and ticks. However, the echidna would seem to have a problem. How do you groom yourself when you're covered in rows and rows of long, prickly spines? The answer is with long, pointed claws! The second claw on each of the echidna's back feet is an extra-long grooming claw. This is used to help the echidna clean between its spines.

△ Good memory
Echidnas have a highly developed cerebral cortex. This is the area of the brain responsible for attention and memory. They are therefore believed to be able to make good mental maps for navigating around their territory.

▷ Cooling down
Short-beaked echidnas don't have sweat glands and can't pant to cool down. To avoid overheating, they will usually shelter amid foliage or in burrows or hollow trees during the hottest part of the day.

Tarsier

Scientific Name: Genus *Tarsius*

EYES
These huge eyes can't move in the socket. To make up for this, tarsiers can rotate their head through almost 180 degrees in both directions, like an owl.

HEAD & BODY
Depending on the subspecies, tarsiers can grow up to 6in (15cm) long. The mammal's back legs are about twice as long as its body.

TEETH
Sharp, stabbing teeth and broad crushing molars tell us that tarsiers have a varied diet that includes everything from insects to birds, to poisonous snakes.

HANDS
The tarsier's hands and feet are long and flexible. Fleshy pads on the tips of the fingers and toes give a better grip.

The tarsier's success as a predator is due to the element of surprise. With its huge eyes and elongated fingers, this cutie might look like something out of a fairy tale, but it's really a rare type of primate. Most primates, including humans, have a varied diet. Tarsiers, though, are completely carnivorous, eating everything from insects to poisonous snakes. When it spots prey, the tarsier leaps into action, bouncing from tree to tree as it chases down its prey. As it jumps, it twists its body in mid-air and extends its long fingers, ready to grab hold of the next tree. The tarsier's elongated ankle bones act like shock absorbers to prevent injuries as it bounds along.

ACTUAL SIZE

▷ THESE SHY CREATURES spend much of their time in the treetops, hidden amid the foliage. From there it is easy to spot prey. This hungry predator has just seen something tasty fly by. Using the tree trunk like a launch pad, the tarsier springs from tree to tree. It is so fast that the butterfly doesn't have a chance of escaping. Settling down to enjoy its meal, the successful hunter scans the forest for more potential meals. All that leaping about burns a lot of energy, so this tarsier will need more than one butterfly to keep its body fueled up.

Where in the world?

Tarsiers are found on many of the islands of southeast Asia. They make their homes in dense bamboo forests, rainforests, and plantations, where they use the foliage to stay well hidden.

Did you know?

- Tarsiers get their name from their long tarsus (ankle) bones. These bones give them their distinctive long legs.

- Tarsiers can leap over 6ft (1.8m) in a single bound.

- The tarsier's body is so well adapted to leaping that it finds it hard to walk. Instead, tarsiers hop around like an oversized furry frog.

- Only one baby tarsier is born at a time. They are born well developed, with open eyes and fur. Within two days of being born the baby is able to climb. By day four it has learned to jump.

- Tarsiers have the largest eyes in proportion to body size of any mammal.

PHOTOFILE: Tarsier

▷ **Useful tail**
While in the treetops, the tarsier wraps its tail around the branch to help it keep an upright posture. The tail is naked (except for a tuft of hair at the tip) and the underside is ridged for added grip.

FACT

These adorable creatures are arboreal (they live in or among trees). During the day, they hide in tree hollows or at the base of a tree, amid roots and foliage. It is only at night that they come out to hunt. Because of this, very little is known about their habits although, in common with many primates, it is believed that they live in tight-knit family groups. Within these groups the female seems to be solely responsible for caring for the young.

△ **Ancient family**
These odd animals are the
descendants of an ancient line
of primates that can be traced
back 55.8–33.9 million years. Like
all primates, they have forward-
facing eyes, dextrous hands, and
a large brain to body mass.

▷ **Enormous eyes**
Each of this little primate's huge
eyes measures around ¹⁄₂in (1.2cm) in
diameter. Amazingly, that means that the
volume of its eye sockets is bigger than
both its brain case and its stomach.

Grasshopper Mouse

Scientific Name: Genus *Onychomys*

BODY
Short legs and a stocky body mean that the grasshopper mouse isn't a fast runner but, when attacking prey, it is both agile and daring.

FUR
The fur of the grasshopper mouse is generally gray-brown or reddish-brown in color. The exact color varies from species to species and region to region.

TAIL
This mouse's tail is short and stubby. In comparison, the tail of the house mouse is often as long as or longer than its body.

FINGERS
The mouse's fingers and claws are particularly long. This is an adaptation to its predatory lifestyle, as it allows the mouse to easily grasp and manipulate prey.

Whether it's a scorpion, tarantula, or a poisonous millipede, the tiny grasshopper mouse (genus *Onychomys*) is a match for all comers. While most mice eat seeds, the grasshopper mouse is a carnivore, feeding on insects, other small rodents, lizards, and snakes. This hunter may have the body of mouse, but it has the heart and soul of a wolf. It even howls at the moon before settling down to crunch into its prey! Moving with surprising agility, the grasshopper mouse uses both cunning and natural abilities to kill large and poisonous insects and arachnids without being killed itself. Strong legs, long claws, sharp teeth, as well as an immunity to some poisons makes this little predator a big success story.

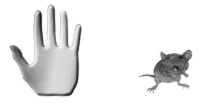

ACTUAL SIZE

▷ IN BEHAVIOR, the grasshopper mouse is more like wolf than a rodent. It forms family packs, defends large territories, and even howls like a wolf while standing on its back legs. Like the wolf, the grasshopper mouse is a clever hunter. Much of its prey is either poisonous or as big as itself, so it has developed techniques for dealing with each animal. When hunting other rodents, it kills with a bite to the back of the neck, but poisonous prey needs special care. In a series of fast hit-and-run attacks, the mouse bites off the stinger first then safely consumes the scorpion.

Where in the world?

The northern grasshopper mouse is found from central Canada to northern Mexico. The southern grasshopper mouse occupies southern California to northeastern Mexico. Mearns' grasshopper mouse ranges from southwest United States to central Mexico.

Did you know?

● The grasshopper mouse also feeds on stink beetles, which are famous for spraying attackers with a foul-smelling toxic liquid from their rear ends. The grasshopper mouse deals with the problem by pushing the beetle's backside into the earth. Having done this, it can munch down the rest of the beetle's body in safety.

● This mouse prefers low, dry sandy desert areas, where it lives in burrows that it either digs itself or steals from other rodents.

● A young grasshopper mouse is called a pinkie, kitten, or pup. Females are called does and males are known as bucks. A group of grasshopper mice is called a nest, colony, harvest, horde, or mischief.

● Rodents like the grasshopper mouse make up 40 percent of all known mammal species.

PHOTOFILE: Grasshopper Mouse

▷ **The clawed mouse**
The grasshopper mouse belongs to the scientific group *Onychomys*. This means "clawed mouse," in reference to their extra-long claws. *Onychomys* is specifically a "New World" genus, so is found only in the Americas.

FACT

Despite appearances, the grasshopper mouse is not closely related to the house mouse. Most rodents have a single pair of upper and lower incisors that grow continuously. Mice must gnaw continuously to stop their teeth growing too long, and this gnawing gives them a chisel-like shape. The grasshopper mouse's incisors are not broad, slicing tools but narrow, piercing daggers. These stabbing, tearing teeth allows them to tackle a much wider range of prey.

△ **Howling at the moon**
Perhaps it is their way of
advertising their hunting
prowess to rivals and possible
mates? Or perhaps they are just
making a territorial claim? The
truth is, we simply don't know why
grasshopper mice howl at the moon!

▷ **A varied menu**
This little hunter's prey varies widely
depending on its habitat. Some grasshopper
mice survive almost entirely on a diet of bugs
and beetles; others prey on rodents such as
prairie voles and cotton rats.

Jaguar

Scientific Name: *Panthera onca*

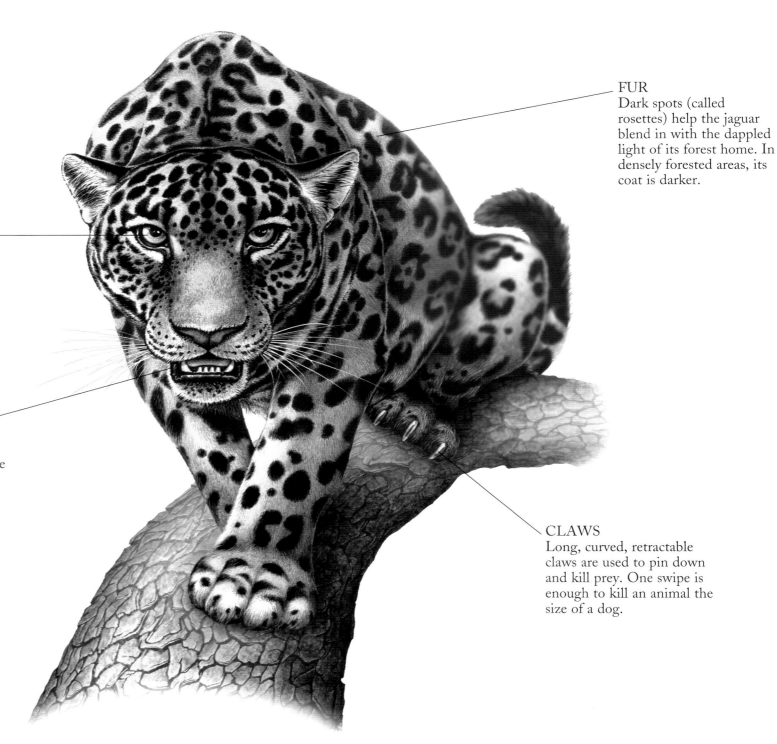

FUR
Dark spots (called rosettes) help the jaguar blend in with the dappled light of its forest home. In densely forested areas, its coat is darker.

EYES
A mirror-like structure at the back of the eye (the tapetum lucidum) reflects light into the retina. This gives cats better vision in low light.

JAWS
Most big cats kill with a bite to the throat. The jaguar's jaws are so strong that it can also kill its victims by piercing the prey's skull.

CLAWS
Long, curved, retractable claws are used to pin down and kill prey. One swipe is enough to kill an animal the size of a dog.

Champion predators need to be powerful and flexible, and jaguars (*Panthera onca*) are just that. Although they look similar to leopards, they're shorter, stockier, and much stronger. A jaguar can drag an 800lb (362kg) bull in their jaws and crush its bones with ease! They're most at home in the rainforest where prey includes tree-dwelling monkeys and water-bound caiman, but they are adaptable. In areas close to human settlements, they use their eyesight, hearing, and sense of smell to hunt when it's dark. In more rural regions, they hunt in the half-lit twilight world just before the dawn. All of these factors puts the jaguar at the top of the South American food chain.

ACTUAL SIZE

▷ In the rainforest, a big cat like a jaguar would struggle if it had to chase prey through the tangled undergrowth. Instead it uses a stalk-and-ambush technique. Creeping up silently on its prey, it's only when its target is almost close enough to touch that the cat strikes. Moving with surprising speed, the jaguar takes its victim completely by surprise. The jaguar usually suffocates its prey with a bite to the throat, but also uses a unique killing method. Using its powerful jaws like a nutcracker, it crunches through the bones of the skull, piercing the brain.

Did you know?

● It is believed that ancestors of the modern-day jaguar evolved such powerful jaws so that they could take advantage of the armored turtles that were common during the Pleistocene period, 2,588,000 to 11,700 years ago. When the turtles became extinct, jaguars began to hunt other animals.

● One of the native names for this powerful cat is *yaguareté*. This means "true fierce beast."

● The rosettes on the jaguar's coat are different on each cat. Some rosettes may include one or more dots, and their shape, size, and color vary.

● Ancient South America myths all tell stories of jaguar gods and spirits. The Aztecs also dressed their best warriors as jaguars because they believed that this would give them the animal's strength and power during battles.

Where in the world?

Although they were once common throughout the Americas, jaguars are now mainly found in Brazil, Paraguay, and Belize. They are an adaptable species, but prefer to live in wet woodlands or flooded, marshy areas.

PHOTOFILE: Jaguar

▷ **Looking for prey**
A tree makes a good vantage point.
Here, above the forest floor, the
jaguar can look for prey without
being seen. It is also a great place to
launch an attack, and many jaguars
do just that.

FACT

**Jaguars belong to the
scientific group (genus)
Panthera. Within this group
only the jaguar, the tiger,
the lion, and the leopard can
roar. This is because they
have a specially enlarged
larynx and hyoid bone
(located in the neck). The
bigger the larynx is, the
louder the cat can roar.
This is why the lion has
the most impressive roar of
all the big cats. Strangely,
though, the cougar, cheetah,
and the snow leopard can't
roar, although their larynx
is similar.**

△ **Eyes of a killer**
Adult jaguars have eyes that vary in color from a striking golden-yellow to a more orangey hue. However, jaguar cubs are born with blue eyes that change color after two or three months.

▷ **River swimmer**
Not every cat hates water. Jaguars not only like water, but they spend a lot of time in and around rivers, where they prey on fish, turtles, and other reptiles. They are surprisingly good swimmers.

Polar Bear

Scientific Name: *Ursus maritimus*

BODY
The polar bear's closest relative is the brown bear. The species look similar, but the polar bear has a more elongated body and a longer head.

BLUBBER
Up to 4in (10cm) of blubber lies beneath this thick fur coat. This protects the bear from the extreme cold of its Arctic home.

CLAWS
The bottom of the polar bear's feet are furry, giving extra grip. Curved claws do the same job, allowing the bear to be surprisingly agile on slippery surfaces.

PAWS
The bear's large, wide paws act like a pair of snowshoes. They spread the animal's weight so that it doesn't fall through the ice.

The polar bear (*Ursus maritimus*) is the world's largest land-based carnivore. In fact, a male polar bear is twice the size of a Siberian tiger! This incredible creature spends its life in the most northern part of our planet: the Arctic. Here, temperatures can fall as low as −90°F (−68 °C) and the sea freezes over. However, this bear is superbly adapted to survive such extremes. A thick layer of blubber beneath the skin keeps it warm. Huge paws and curved claws help it

ACTUAL SIZE

to move around on the ice. An excellent sense of smell allows it to sniff out food under 36in (91cm) of snow. It even has slightly webbed toes for swimming between ice floes in search of prey.

▷ SPOTTING A GROUP of seals on the opposite shore, the polar bear silently slips into the water. The temperature is well below freezing, but, protected by that big fur coat, the bear barely notices the chill. Seals are slow and clumsy on land. Although its companions managed to slip safely into the water, this seal has left it too late to make a getaway. Rearing up on its hind legs, the bear lashes out. Its paws are so powerful that the seal is killed instantly. Now all the bear has to do is drag the seal's body somewhere safe where it can eat undisturbed.

Where in the world?

The polar bear's scientific name means "marine bear," because it spends many months of the year at sea. It lives in the Arctic Circle and on the sea ice that covers the waters during the winter.

Did you know?

● Polar bears have black skins and colorless hair. Every hair is actually a hollow "tube" and any light that enters the tube is scattered, so it appears white.

● Bears may turn green in warm weather when algae starts to grow inside their hollow hairs!

● Although temperatures in the Arctic are well below freezing, the bear's fur and blubber are so good at keeping out the chill that they can overheat.

● The polar bear has a much longer neck than other bears. This is an adaptation that allows them to keep their head above water while swimming.

PHOTOFILE: Polar Bear

▷ **Polar bear cubs**
Bear cubs are usually born in December or January. Although adult bears are an impressive sight, newborns are furless, blind, and deaf. They stay safe with their mother in their den until March or April.

FACT
Polar bears are classed as a "vulnerable" species. The biggest threat to their continued survival is climate change. These big carnivores have adapted to survive almost exclusively on a diet of seal blubber, catching their prey when it surfaces on blocks of sea ice. Warmer temperatures mean that the sea ice melts earlier and earlier every year, leaving the bears to starve. Some scientists believe that polar bears could be extinct within 100 years.

△ Specialized teeth
Polar bears have 42 teeth, all
of which have a special job
to do. Incisors are used to shear
off blubber and flesh. Canine
teeth are for grasping prey.
Jagged premolars and molars are
used for tear and chewing.

▷ Feasting on blubber
Polar bears need high-energy food.
Fortunately, seal blubber is very high in
calories. When the hunting is good, the bear
will eat only the blubber, leaving the rest of
the carcass for other Arctic scavengers.

American Short-tailed Shrew

Scientific Name: Genus *Blarina*

WHISKERS
Although the shrew's
eyesight is poor, it has
as very keen sense of
smell. Sensitive vibrissae
(whiskers) on its snout
help it locate prey.

FRONT PAWS
Shrews use their front
feet to dig tunnels
for their elaborate
underground burrows.
They are semi-fossorial,
which means that they
spend much of their
time underground.

BODY
The short-tailed
shrew's mouth is
packed with 32 spike-
like teeth. Grooves in
the lower incisor teeth
carries a poison that
can paralyze or kill.

SCENT GLANDS
Scent glands on the
shrew's belly and sides
produce the strong-
smelling liquids that
they use to scent-mark
territory and to help
them to find mates.

The short-tailed shrew is one of the world's few poisonous mammals. It generally eats insects, earthworms, and snails. Its little body needs a lot of fuel. It needs to eat around three times its weight every day or it will starve to death. The shrew is clever, hunting whatever prey is available, including voles, frogs, snakes, and other shrews. Grooves in the shrew's lower incisor teeth carry the poison, which enters the victim through saliva. This poison is a specialized neurotoxin powerful enough to paralyze small prey for up to 15 days at a time. This allows the shrew to stockpile its food and, because the paralyzed prey is still alive, there is no worry about it spoiling.

A C T U A L   S I Z E

▷ THERE'S A WELL-KNOWN proverb that "curiosity killed the cat," meaning that sometimes it can be dangerous to be too curious. This little boy needs to be careful in case his curiosity gets him into trouble! Although shrews usually hunt under cover of darkness, on cloudy days, hunger can force them out of their burrows to find food. Kneeling down to take a closer look at the shrew, the boy cups his hands around the little animal's body. He doesn't mean any harm, but the shrew doesn't know that! Its bite won't kill, but it can cause a very painful wound.

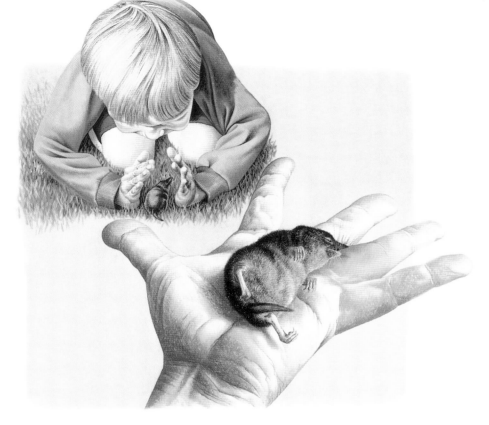

Where in the world?

The northern short-tailed shrew, southern short-tailed shrew, Elliot's short-tailed shrew, and the Everglades short-tailed shrew can all be found in North America. They live in many different habitats but like wet areas with thick vegetation.

Did you know?

● Short-tailed shrews belong to a group known as red-toothed shrews. The enamel on the tips of the shrew's teeth contains an iron pigment. As the teeth wear down, the pigment is exposed to the air and turns red.

● Shrews may look like mice, but they are more closely related to moles.

● Many predators learn to avoid eating shrews because of the offensive smells produced by the animal's strong scent glands.

● If the shrew swallows some of its own poisoned saliva, it is destroyed by stomach acids before it can do any damage. However, if one shrew bites another during a fight, the bite could be fatal.

● One of the ingredients that make up the shrew's poison is being investigated as a possible anticancer drug.

PHOTOFILE: American Short-tailed Shrew

▷ **Thick fur**
Short-tailed shrews have a thick coat of brown or gray fur, a pointed snout, and large, fleshy hands and feet. Their ears are completely hidden beneath their fur, and their tiny dark eyes are almost invisible.

FACT

Short-tailed shrews have very poor eyesight. They make up for this by using a form of echolocation. The shrew makes a high-pitched squeak and listens to the returning echoes to build up a picture of its surroundings. The shrew's echolocation is not as sensitive or as sophisticated as that used by toothed whales or microbats. However, it is still a very useful tool to have when it comes to tracking down and catching prey.

△ Sociable shrews
Elliot's short-tailed shrew
(*Blarina hylophaga*) is a solitary
animal, but members of the
southern short-tailed shrew family
(*Blarina carolinensis*) are much more
sociable. These furry little critters
sometimes share their burrow with
several other shrews.

▷ Hunting paths
This little mammal is a nocturnal hunter
that spends much of the day asleep in
its burrow. A network of regularly used
pathways leads from the burrow entrance to
the areas where the shrew usually hunts.

Stoat

Scientific Name: *Mustela erminea*

FUR
A stoat's winter fur is thick and silky. Its summer coat is much rougher. The fur of stoats in the far north turns white in the winter.

TAIL
Stoats and least weasels (*Mustela nivalis*) look very similar. However, stoats have a black tip on the end of their tail, and least weasels don't.

BODY
The stoat's body is streamlined. Its long, thin shape, narrow skull, and ears set close to the head help it hunt in underground burrows.

PAWS
Each of the feet has five toes tipped with long, sharp claws. These claws help the stoat to keep its grip when climbing up trees.

With its cute looks and comic way of bounding about, the stoat (*Mustela erminea*) makes an adorable sight, but watch out! This cuddly critter has claws and teeth and knows how to use them. The stoat may be small but it is a superbly skillful hunter. Its body is designed for squeezing into tight spaces and its superb sense of smell allows it to easily sniff out prey in underground burrows. It is an excellent climber and will steal birds eggs straight from the nest. It will even fish in shallow waters if it is given the chance. However, it is above ground that the stoat excels. It will eat anything from birds to lizards but particularly likes rabbits, despite the fact that most rabbits are at least twice its size.

ACTUAL SIZE

▷ STOATS ARE CUNNING hunters, making use of natural cover such as shrubs or walls to get close to their prey. As rabbits are fast and easy to startle, it takes practice to get this good. With one bound, the stoat leaps onto the rabbit's back, sinking its needle-like teeth into its prey's neck. Although the rabbit is hurt, instinct takes over. With a bound, the rabbit is off, running for its life. The stoat doesn't give chase. It knows from experience that, having lost so much blood, the rabbit will not be able to survive. It just doesn't know it yet.

Where in the world?

Stoats are listed as one of the world's 100 most invasive species. They have spread to almost every part of the globe from the Arctic Circle to the Indian subcontinent.

Did you know?

● Although female stoats take at least six weeks to grow to adulthood size, they can breed at just one to two months old!

● Male stoats are called dogs, hobs, or jacks. Females are called bitches or jills. A group of stoats is known as a gang or a pack.

● Stoats line their nests with fur and vegetation along with feathers taken from their prey.

● Of all the strange stories surrounding stoats one includes the belief that they are able to "freeze" a rabbit in its tracks with a hypnotic dance!

PHOTOFILE: Stoat

▷ **Length and size**
On average, male stoats measure between 8–12in (20–30cm) from nose to rump. Females are usually about half the size of their male counterparts. The distinctive black-tipped tail adds another 3–5in (7.5–12.5cm).

FACT

The British author and explorer Sir Alfred Pease (1857–1939) described being attacked by a pack of stoats. They "leaped at him red-eyed, snapping little white fangs, leaping, dancing, darting, as agile as snakes on four legs." Sir Alfred tried to beat the stoats off with his walking stick, but every time they were knocked away, more would come to attack him. He eventually decided to give up the fight and run for his life!

△ **Getting a better look**
Stoats are naturally curious
animals. While they are out
hunting they will often stop,
raise their head, and stand
upright on their back legs so
that they can get a better view
of the surrounding area.

▷ **Storing food**
To stay well and warm, stoats need to
eat every day. When the hunting is good,
they may store excess food in special
"caches" (hiding places) so that they have
enough to eat when prey is scarce.

Tasmanian Devil

Scientific Name: *Sarcophilus harrisii*

BODY
Devils are the largest marsupial, growing up to 31in (79cm). Their front legs are longer than their back legs, giving them a waddling walk.

TAIL
Healthy Tasmanian devils have fat tails because this is where the animal stores excess fat. This fat acts as a food reserve when prey is scarce.

FRONT PAWS
The Tasmanian devil's front paws have four long toes and one "thumb." This allows the marsupial to handle and manipulate its food.

MOUTH
When it is threatened, the Tasmanian devil will often open its mouth in a huge, gaping yawn that shows off its sharp, strong teeth.

Early European settlers were so alarmed by the guttural growls and fierce nature of this marsupial that they dubbed it the Tasmanian "devil" (*Sarcophilus harrisii*). The devil is strong and stocky. It has a reputation as a scavenger, rather than a proper hunter, and it will eat almost anything, including road kill. The devil is also an adaptable and formidable predator. Its oversized head and powerful jaws give it one of the most powerful bites of any animal its size. Its long whiskers and excellent sense of smell allow it to track down prey in complete darkness. Long claws are used to dig burrows and climb trees. Its powerful upper body provides the strength to kill prey as big as itself.

ACTUAL SIZE

▷ DEVILS ARE ARGUMENTATIVE animals and live fairly solitary lives. After they leave their mother's care they will spend much of their time alone. However, they do form loose social networks with other devils in their area. Devils are nocturnal and crepuscular hunters, heading off to find food at night or during dusk and dawn. Unusually, although they live and hunt alone, they seem to enjoy eating in company. In fact, the blood-chilling calls that they make have been interpreted by some scientists as being dinner invitations! The bigger the kill, the louder the cries become.

Did you know?

• The Tasmanian devil was the inspiration for a well-known Looney Tunes cartoon character called Taz. Although Taz looks nothing like a true Tasmanian devil, his loud, aggressive personality is just like the real thing!

• Although Tasmanian devils can run at speeds up to 22mph (35km/h) for short periods, they are built for the marathon rather than the sprint. They can keep up a pace of around 7mph (11km/h) up for several miles.

• Young Tasmanian devils are called pups, joeys, or imps.

• The first Australian settlers ate Tasmanian devils. Apparently their meat tasted like veal.

• Devils are fussy housekeepers! Their dens are kept meticulously clean, with new bedding material regularly brought in to replace any old or damp foliage.

Where in the world?

Once found throughout Australia, Tasmanian devils now live only on the island of Tasmania. Most animals live in very specific habitats, but devils are found all over the island, although they prefer scrublands and forests.

PHOTOFILE: Tasmanian Devil

▷ **Unusual marsupial**
Australia was isolated from other continents for 80 million years. There, marsupials (pouched mammals) like the Tasmanian devil and the monotremes (egg-laying mammals) became dominant.

FACT

The Tasmanian devil's scientific name, *Sarcophilus harrisii* means, "Harris' meat-eater." True to its name, this greedy devil will eat any meat, including birds, snakes, and even human corpses, although its favorite food is wombat. Like most predators, Tasmanian devils will gorge on food when it is plentiful, storing any excess calories as fat. In fact, one devil can eat up to 40 percent of its own body weight in meat in just half an hour!

△ **Precious teeth**
Inside these vicious jaws
are 42 teeth. Unlike many
animals, which have extra
teeth to replace those that
wear out, devils have only one
set. If they wear out too soon
the devil may starve to death.

▷ **Developing fur**
Baby Tasmanian devils remain pink and
furless until they are 50 days old. Fur
starts to grow at the snout and spreads
outward, over the whole body, with the
backside the last part to be covered.

Amphibians & Reptiles

When scientists began to try to sort animals into groups, they placed reptiles, such as snakes, and amphibians, such as frogs, together in the same Class. The thinking was that any creature that wasn't a bird or a mammal was a reptile!

In fact, reptiles and amphibians do have many similarities. While mammals generally have fur and give birth to live young, both snakes and frogs lack fur and usually lay eggs. Today, though, we know that reptiles and amphibians are very different—and this difference is more than skin deep. The clue lies in the word "amphibian." Amphibian means "both kinds of life." That's because amphibians start life in the water and, as they grow, their bodies slowly change in preparation for a life on land. Reptiles don't do this.

However, although reptiles and amphibians live very different lives, they share a love of meat. Most reptiles and all adult amphibians are carnivores and must hunt and kill to live. Some, like the western diamondback rattlesnake, come equipped with potent poison. Others, like the mugger crocodile, use their powerful jaws and bulky bodies to grab prey, which they drag down into the watery depths and drown. Even the harmless-looking leatherback turtle is a voracious hunter that migrates 6,000 miles (9,700km) across the Pacific Ocean every year to gorge on jellyfish!

Oriental Whip Snake

Scientific Name: *Ahaetulla prasina*

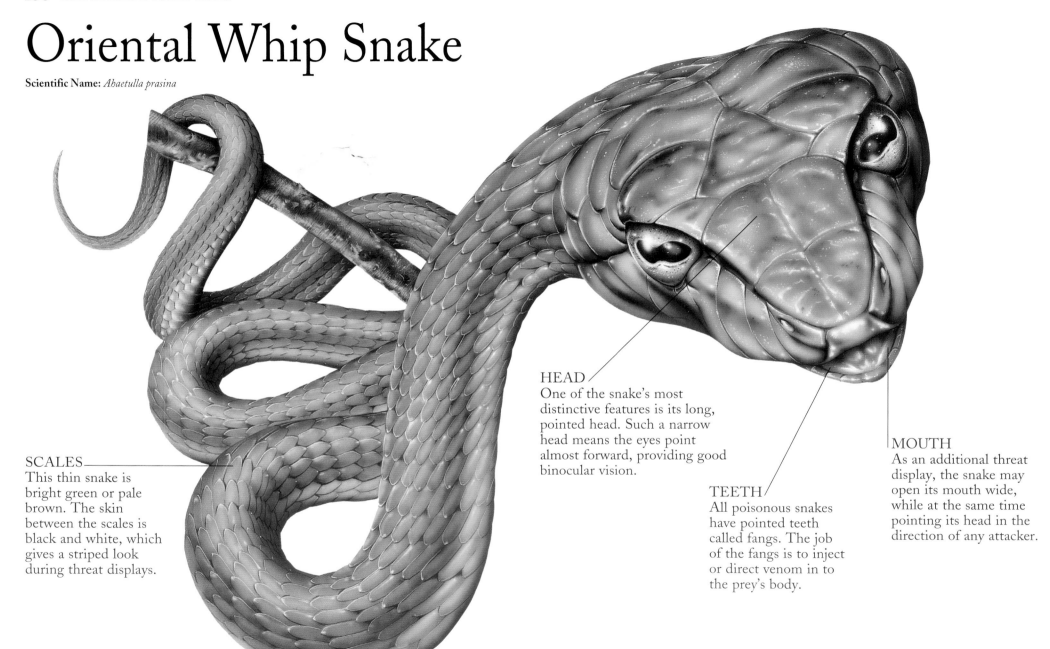

HEAD
One of the snake's most distinctive features is its long, pointed head. Such a narrow head means the eyes point almost forward, providing good binocular vision.

MOUTH
As an additional threat display, the snake may open its mouth wide, while at the same time pointing its head in the direction of any attacker.

TEETH
All poisonous snakes have pointed teeth called fangs. The job of the fangs is to inject or direct venom in to the prey's body.

SCALES
This thin snake is bright green or pale brown. The skin between the scales is black and white, which gives a striped look during threat displays.

Say the word snake and most of us will conjure up images of a deadly cobra or a big, powerful python. However, although the oriental whip snake (*Ahaetulla prasina*) may not be as toxic or as muscular as its relatives, it does have one great advantage when it comes to hunting—stealth! That long, thin, startlingly green body has evolved over millennia to blend in with its surroundings. Resting in its natural habitat, the snake looks exactly like a vine wrapped around a tree branch.

ACTUAL SIZE

This cunning camouflage allows it to get very close to its prey before striking with speed and accuracy. It is so successful at what it does that it can feed on nesting birds, tree lizards, and frogs with ease.

▷ BEING ABLE TO BLEND in with your surroundings is a great advantage for any hunter. The leopard's spots may look brash and bold when you see the animal in a zoo. But, in the low light of a forest clearing, all those reds, blacks, and yellows look like part of the scenery. The same is true for the oriental vine snake. These handsome snakes make popular pets and in a reptile cage their bright green coloring really stands out. Yet here in the forest, the snake can slither through the foliage, almost invisible, until it is ready to make a kill!

Where in the world?

These bright and colorful tree snakes are found in India and China and throughout much of southeast Asia including forested regions of the Philippines, Indonesia, Sri Lanka, Burma, Thailand, Cambodia, and Vietnam.

Did you know?

● Whip snakes grow up to 6ft (1.8m), with a 24in (61cm) tail.

● It used to be believed that the whip snake used its pointed head to blind its victims. We now know that that is not true.

● Günther's whip snake feeds on fish. The snake wraps the bottom half of its body around a branch overhanging a river while its head strikes at fish in water below.

● Most snakes lay eggs. Oriental whip snakes are viviparous, which means that they give birth to live young. These grow within the mother's body inside an egg membrane.

● The name for a baby snake depends on how they are born. Live-born snakes are known as snakelets or neonates. If they come from an egg, they are called hatchlings.

PHOTOFILE: Oriental Whip Snake

▷ **Moving along branches**
The whip snake's long, thin body is the ideal shape for slithering along tree branches. At rest, adults tend to lie across tree branches while smaller, juvenile snakes often wrap themselves around the branch.

FACT

The whip snake has two distinctive features that set it apart from all other snakes. The first are its keyhole-shaped pupils. While most reptiles have small circles or slits for pupils, this keyhole shape helps to widen the snake's binocular field. Two grooves that run along either side of the reptile's snout, from its eyes to its mouth, also help to improve vision. They do this by extending the snake's eyeline for sighting prey.

△ **Swaying snake**
Whip snakes sometimes sway their bodies in windy weather, like a branch being buffeted by the elements. If they are touched, they may fall to the ground and lie motionless like a broken twig!

▷ **Poison fangs**
Generally, poisonous snakes have their fangs at the front of their upper jaw so that they can easily inject their victims with venom. The whip snake's fangs are at the back of its upper jaw, instead.

South American Rattlesnake

Scientific Name: *Crotalus durissus*

EYES
Snakes do not have eyelids or eyelashes. Instead, their eyes are protected from damage by special clear scales that are known as the brille.

PIT ORGAN
This snake is a pit viper. The name comes from the heat-sensing pit organ, which is located between the snake's eyes and its nostrils.

SCALES
Snake skin is covered in rough, dry scales. Snakes like the rattlesnake move using a series of specialized scales on their belly that grip the ground.

JAW
Snakes cannot bite and do not have claws to tear their food. Flexible jaws and movable skull bones allow them to swallow prey whole.

Lying patiently in wait for prey to wander past, the South American rattlesnake (*Crotalus durissus*) is a silent, deadly assassin. These reptiles hunt at night and can detect prey even on dark, moonless evenings. Its secret is those deep holes just under its eyes called "loreal pits." They may look like nostrils, but they're actually the openings for a pair of infrared-detecting organs that enable the snake to "see" the heat given off by the bodies of its prey. Once it is close enough to strike, the snake snaps open its mouth, allowing its long, retractable fangs to spring forward. Those fangs inflict more than just a flesh wound; they also inject the prey (mostly mammals) with deadly poison.

ACTUAL SIZE

▷ THIS GARDENER IS about to have a very nasty surprise! Snakes are shy creatures and will usually hide from humans. However, this snake has chosen a poor hiding place. A rake in the face causes the snake to lash out, biting the man in the ankle. Rattlesnake bites are rarely fatal to humans, but can cause pain, swelling, bleeding, sickness, blindness, and heart failure. Whether this man survives depends on how quickly he can get treatment and how the snake is feeling. If it has just eaten, and is feeling full and lazy, it may not even inject its "attacker" with poison.

Where in the world?

These rattlesnakes are found in every South American country except Ecuador and Chile. They prefer grasslands, but can be found in the Brazilian caatinga (regions of thorny shrubs) and the wetlands and forests of the "cerrado."

Did you know?

- Pit vipers vary in size from the smallest hump-nosed viper, which grows to around 20in (51cm), to the bushmaster, which can reach 12ft (3.6m) in length.

- Rattlesnake skins are often used in South American tribal medicines. This doesn't harm the snake because they shed their skin as they grow.

- As their bodies are long and thin, a snake's paired organs (like kidneys) are positioned one in front of the other, rather than side by side, which is the more usual layout for mammals.

- Female pit vipers are usually larger than the male of the species.

- Gamblers who get a pair of ones in dice games are said to have rolled "snake eyes." This is because of the association between snakes and bad luck.

PHOTOFILE: South American Rattlesnake

▷ **Sheltering from the heat**
Rattlesnakes are most active during the warmer months of the year. However, as they can't regulate their body heat they will often take cover under shrubs or rocks during the hottest part of the day.

FACT

Rattlesnakes are one of the easiest species of snake to recognize thanks to their tail rattle. Even babies are born with the beginnings of a rattle, known as a pre-button. As the snake grows, it sheds its skin. After the baby's first shedding it gets the first real segment of rattle, called a button. Snakes shed their skin one to four times a year; an extra segment is added to the rattle with every shedding.

△ **Forked tongue**
Many reptiles have a tongue
that is split at the end (known
as "forked"). Reptiles use their
tongue to smell, and a forked
tongue has more surface area
to detect the scent-carrying
particles in the air.

▷ **The rattlesnake's rattle**
The snake's rattle is hollow. Its distinctive
sound is made by the segments of the
rattle bumping against one other as the
tail is shaken. The rattle is fairly brittle
and segments can break off.

Colorado River Toad

Scientific Name: *Bufo alvarius*

SKIN
The dark brown-olive green skin is shiny and smooth. The belly is much paler in color—almost white. The toad's skin is also toxic.

BODY
The bulbous body grows to 7½in (19cm) long, making the Colorado River toad the largest native American toad. (The non-native cane toad is bigger.)

EYES
Eyes on the top of their head allow the toad to keep a look out above and below while their body is under the water's surface.

PARATOID GLANDS
Colorado River toads have enlarged glands, called paratoid glands, on the side of the neck and behind each eye. These produce a thick, white poison.

This big amphibian has a big appetite; little escapes America's largest native toad. Inside that massive mouth is a long tongue with a sticky tip, used to catch small insects. For larger prey like rodents, lizards, and other amphibians, the toad uses its muscular front legs to grab food and stuff it into its mouth. Unlike most amphibians, the Colorado River toad (*Bufo alvarius*) has few enemies—any creature attempting to eat it is likely to end up dead! When the toad is alarmed, parotoid glands under its eyes give off a toxic liquid. Warty bumps by the mouth and on the legs have a similar use, making the Colorado River toad one dangerous amphibian—both to its prey and to other predators!

ACTUAL SIZE

▷ THIS TOAD DOESN'T LOOK very appealing, but there is more to those warty bumps than meets the eye. In fact, they are not warts at all but glands that produce a potentially potent deadly poison. Thinking that the toad might make a tasty treat—or perhaps something fun to play with—this curious dog picks it up and carries it away. The dog soon discovers its mistake and drops the toad, but it is too late. The toad's toxin contains a powerful mix of chemicals that could kill a fully grown dog, unless its owner calls a vet immediately.

Where in the world?

The Colorado River toad is a native of the Colorado River, California. It is also found along the Gila River, which flows into Sonora, Mexico. This is why it is also known as the Sonoran Desert toad.

Did you know?

• Toads don't have teeth, so they swallow their food whole.

• When hunting, the Colorado River toad rapidly wiggles one of its toes. This ploy attracts the interest of other small predators, which mistake the movement for an insect scurrying through the undergrowth. As they come closer to investigate, the toad strikes!

• Male members of the true toad family *Bufonidae* have a Bidder's organ. If the male's sex organs don't work properly, the Bidder's organ turns the he into a she!

• Female river toads lay 7,500–8,000 eggs, which are encased in a long, jelly-like tube.

PHOTOFILE: Colorado River Toad

▷ **Members of the family**
Scientifically speaking, toads are members of the frog order. The label "toad" refers to true toads belonging to the family *Bufonidae*. This widespread group can be found on every continent except Australia, the Arctic, and Antarctic.

FACT

These big, bulky toads are nocturnal and stay underground or sheltered under rocky outcrops during the hottest part of the day. They spend most of the summer months in a burrow that they dig for themselves or otherwise use a convenient, abandoned rodent den. Very little is known about their day-to-day life but, like all amphibians, they lay their eggs in water and will use any convenient source, from temporary pools to animals' watering troughs.

△ Warty skin
The Colorado River toad has many features in common with other true toads. It has short legs, a bulging body, and no tail. Its skin is dry and appears warty, although its "warts" are really parotoid glands.

▷ Motion-detecting eyes
Eyes with slit pupils are especially good at detecting motion. Only carnivores have eyes with vertically slit pupils. In toads, the slits are horizontal (not vertical), which helps them to spot flying prey, like insects.

Australian Copperhead Snake

Scientific Name: Genus *Austrelaps*

SIZE
The three species of Australian copperhead snake vary in size. As its name suggests, the pygmy is the smallest, while the lowlands copperhead is the largest.

COLOR
Although some copperheads do have a copper-colored head, some do not. Color varies from individual to individual and across species, from orange-brown to black.

BODY
Almost all *Elapidae* family snakes have slender bodies, smooth scales, a head that is not always distinct from the neck, and eyes with round pupils.

FANGS
Hollow fangs at the front of the jaw inject prey with poison. Unlike rattlesnake fangs, these teeth are short so don't fold back in the mouth.

The Australian copperhead snake (genus *Austrelaps*) has a poison that is as toxic as that of an India cobra. Yet what makes this snake so successful is its adaptability. From mountainside forests to lowland heaths, all three species of copperhead snake make a living in parts of Australia where other reptiles would struggle to survive. The copperhead can stand much cooler temperatures than other snakes, but can take advantage of whatever prey is available. During the day, it will hunt small ground-dwelling mammals. It can also climb trees to eat birds and lizards when it needs to. At night, it hunts prey under cover of darkness. It will even take to the water to feed on tadpoles and larger amphibians.

ACTUAL SIZE

▷ AUSTRALIAN COPPERHEADS are secretive snakes that prefer to stay hidden. Even if they are accidentally disturbed, they usually give fair warning before attacking. Hissing loudly, the snake will thrash about, trying to look as threatening as possible to drive away any intruder. Unfortunately, this farmer has misunderstood the snake's signals. Rather than staying calm and keeping still, his reaction makes the snake even more nervous. Finally, it lashes out. The farmer makes a run for it, but it may already be too late. The snake's poison can kill unless the victim gets medical help!

Where in the world?

There are three species of Australian copperhead: the pygmy copperhead of southern Australia; the highlands copperhead of New South Wales and Victoria, and the lowlands copperhead, found around New South Wales, South Australia, Tasmania, and Victoria.

Did you know?

● Despite sharing its name with the American copperhead snake, the Australian copperhead is no relation.

● The Australian copperhead's venom is as toxic as that of the well-known Indian cobra. However, there are so many deadly reptiles in Australia that the copperhead counts only as "moderately toxic" when compared to other species of Australasian snake!

● Copperheads have a sneaky trick for attracting prey. They coil up with their head close to their tail. Then they wiggle their tail in the hope that some passing animal will mistake it for a tasty snack and come within striking distance! This is called caudal-luring.

● There are more than 2,900 known species of snakes. They can be found on every continent except the Arctic and Antarctic. Some snakes even live in the sea.

PHOTOFILE: Australian Copperhead Snake

▷ **Sense of hearing**
Although they don't have any obvious ears, snakes can hear—especially low-frequency sounds. Their bodies are also sensitive to vibrations in the air and on the ground, helping them to sense and move toward approaching prey.

FACT

Mammals use food as fuel to keep their bodies warm. Reptiles are cold-blooded and heat their bodies externally. This is why many reptiles bask in the early-morning sun to warm up. However, as they can't regulate their temperature, they are very sensitive to too much or too little heat. As temperatures rise, snakes will stretch their body out to cool down. When temperatures start to drop, they will coil up to preserve body heat.

△ **Periscoping**

Snakes use a technique called periscoping to help spot prey. They do this by raising their head above the surrounding vegetation to look around. Such periscoping is more common in active, fast-moving species.

▷ **Heading**

The snake's tongue is a more sensitive and accurate olfactory (smell) organ than its nose. The flickering tongue picks up scent molecules in the air to be analyzed by the Jacobson's organ on the roof of the mouth.

Cape Cobra

Scientific Name: *Naja nivea*

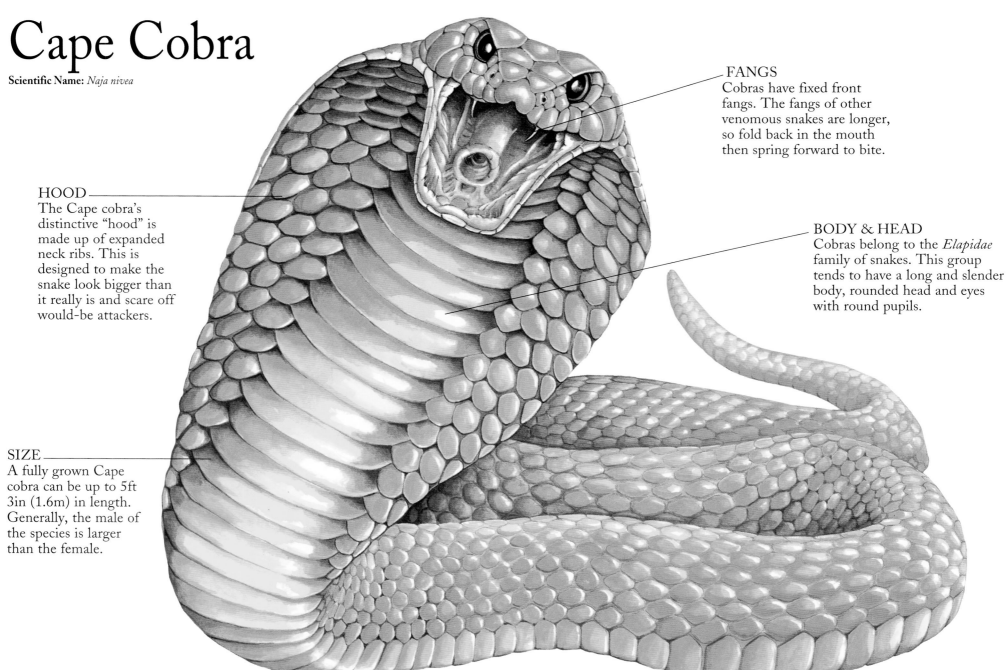

FANGS
Cobras have fixed front fangs. The fangs of other venomous snakes are longer, so fold back in the mouth then spring forward to bite.

HOOD
The Cape cobra's distinctive "hood" is made up of expanded neck ribs. This is designed to make the snake look bigger than it really is and scare off would-be attackers.

BODY & HEAD
Cobras belong to the *Elapidae* family of snakes. This group tends to have a long and slender body, rounded head and eyes with round pupils.

SIZE
A fully grown Cape cobra can be up to 5ft 3in (1.6m) in length. Generally, the male of the species is larger than the female.

The Cape cobra (*Naja nivea*) is a fast, aggressive, and highly toxic snake. The average amount of poison in one bite from a Cape cobra is between 120 and 250 milligrams. Only 15–20 milligrams are needed to kill an adult human, which makes this striking-looking reptile one of Africa's most dangerous species. The cobra's venom is a powerful neurotoxin, which causes paralysis and eventually leads to death. Fortunately people aren't its prey. It much prefers rodents, lizards, and even other Cape cobras! Although it mostly lives on the ground, it is agile enough to climb trees to raid bird's nests. It is also a good swimmer and will happily enter the water to make a meal out of any frogs or toads that it comes across.

ACTUAL SIZE

E In the heat of the day, Cape cobras like to find a cool place to relax. Unfortunately, that causes problems for both snakes and homeowners. Most encounters with snakes in South Africa happen when a snake is in the wrong place at the wrong time! Terrified, the woman backs away from the cobra. What she doesn't know is that the reptile is just as frightened as she is. The raised hood and hissing are both warning signs. The snake simply wants the woman to stay well away. If she remains calm and still then the chances are that the snake will lose interest and slither away.

Where in the world?

Cape cobras live around scrublands and dry desert regions of South Africa's Cape Province, the Free State Province, and in the Transvaal. They are also found from southern Namibia up into the Kalahari Desert.

Did you know?

● No one knows for certain how long Cape cobras live in the wild, but one in San Diego Zoo lived to be more than 15 years old.

● About a million people a year are bitten by snakes. In half of all attacks, the snake doesn't poison the person, because it has no intention of eating them!

● 23 species of snake are found in the Cape Peninsula. Five of these are dangerous, including the puff adder, Berg adder, Cape cobra, ringhals, and boomslang.

● The erect posture and swaying motion that cobras adopt before they attack is said to hypnotize their prey. The truth is that the snake sways as a way of judging the distance between itself and its prey. Its victim is not "entranced"; it is simply too terrified to move.

PHOTOFILE: Cape Cobra

E **Colorful cobra**
The Cape cobra comes in a wide range of colors. In its South African home, it is also known as the geelslang (yellow snake), bruinkapel, (brown cobra), and koperkapel (copper cobra), although they can be almost black.

FACT

There are three types of venomous snake. Solenoglyphous snakes have huge, hollow, movable fangs. Opisthoglyphous snakes have long, movable fangs that are grooved to direct venom into the wound inflicted by the teeth. Proteroglyphous snakes, like cobras, have shorter fangs, fixed in position at the front of the mouth. These fangs are like hollow needles. The snake injects poison directly into its prey by biting and chewing down until the poison has entered its victim's body.

G Adult coloring
This snake is an adult, as shown by its yellowy-colored throat. Juvenile Cape cobras have a dark brown patch on their throat that gradually fades as the snake matures.

E Slit pupils
It is a myth that only snakes with slit pupils are poisonous. Venomous snakes can have round pupils (like the cobra), as well as keyhole-shaped pupils, or pupils that are slit horizontally or vertically.

Russell's Viper

Scientific Name: *Daboia russelii*

HEAD & BODY
Russell's viper has a very broad, triangular-shaped head. Its body is thick and muscular, growing up to 5ft 6in (1.7m) long.

SNOUT
Pit vipers have distinct "pits" between their eyes and nostrils. Russell's viper belongs to a different snake group (called the Viperinae) that lack pit organs.

FANGS
Russell's vipers have two "active" fangs and up to six pairs of replacement fangs that sit in the lower jaw. If a fang breaks or wears out, a replacement takes its place, but it doesn't become active (able to deliver venom) until it locks in place in the jaw.

W hen this snake coils its body into an S-shape, rears up and starts to hiss, watch out. Russell's viper is a snake that is quick to anger and just as quick to bite! Between 40 and 70 milligrams of viper venom is usually enough to kill a fully grown adult, and this snake injects up to 112 milligrams of poison in a single bite. Luckily, Russell's viper (*Daboia russelii*) is not a man-eater. Most of its encounters with humans are accidental, as it often slips into homes in search of rats and mice. Like most snakes, this viper eats its prey whole. To do this, its jaws flip open on "elastic" ligaments, while muscle ripples force its victim's corpse down the viper's throat.

ACTUAL SIZE

E IT IS NO SURPRISE that farmers in India live in fear of this big, muscular snake. Russell's viper is one of Asia's most dangerous snakes. Unfortunately, it loves slithering around farms and in farm buildings, where the pickings are easy. This snake is looking for a quick meal and is alarmed by the farmer coming along to collect eggs. Biting down on the farmer's hand, the viper holds on, pumping venom into its victim. The effects of the poison can be felt almost at once. The bite is painful and swollen, but kidney failure and even death may occur if the farmer doesn't get help quickly.

Where in the world?

These colorful vipers are widespread throughout most of the Indian subcontinent as well as China, Taiwan, and Indonesia. They generally avoid rainforests and marshy areas, but will occupy any other habitats where food is plentiful.

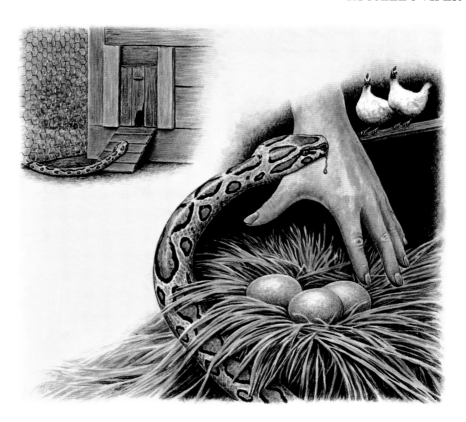

Did you know?

• The poison from Russell's viper makes blood clot. Amazingly, this destructive toxin can also be used for good. A diluted version of the venom can stop uncontrolled bleeding in people suffering from hemophilia.

• Russell's viper is named after the Scottish naturalist Patrick Russell (1726–1805), who did much of his work in India.

• The species' scientific name, *Daboia*, comes from a Hindi phrase meaning "the lurker."

• The biggest known litter of baby Russell's vipers was 65!

• In Aesop's fable of "The Farmer and the Viper," a farmer finds a viper freezing in the snow and puts it under his coat to warm it up. The viper revives and bites his rescuer. The moral of the tale is that kindness to evil is always met with evil.

PHOTOFILE: Russell's Viper

E **Spotting prey**
Most vipers have vertically slit pupils. This design allows them see in a wide range of light conditions. It also widens their binocular field on the horizontal plane, helping them spot moving prey on the ground.

FACT

Lying scattered amid the parched grass, this viper is almost invisible thanks to its incredible camouflage. Some camouflages use mimesis, where one object "mimics" another. The most common form of mimesis is where a harmless animal has evolved to look like a more dangerous species. Crypsis is a type of camouflage that allows an object to blend in with its surroundings. Russell's viper uses its "cryptic" camouflage to remain hidden while it is hunting prey.

G Milking venom
A snake is "milked" for its venom. The venom is then diluted and injected into another animal. The animal's body produces antibodies that can be used to produce an antivenom to counteract the effects of the poison.

E Dangerous snakes
Russell's viper is one of Asia's "big four" snakes—those that are responsible for the most attacks on humans. The other three are the Indian cobra, the common krait, and the saw-scaled viper.

Red-eyed Tree Frog

Scientific Name: *Agalychnis callidryas*

EYES
This frog's huge, bulging, red eyes are its most obvious feature. The frog has three eyelids. The third eyelid is called the nictitating membrane. This membrane allows the frog to shield its eyes from danger while still being able to see.

FEET
The tree frog's feet are large and flexible. Sticky pads on its digits help it to grip onto foliage. The frog's partially webbed feet help it to swim.

TONGUE
The long, thin tongue has a sticky tip that is used like a fishing rod to catch the tree frog's victims and reel them in.

By day, this startlingly colorful frog stays out of sight, sleeping on the underside of leaves, with its eyes closed and its blue flashes hidden by its feet. At night, when its bright green coloration is shrouded in darkness, it comes out to feed. The red-eyed tree frog (*Agalychnis callidryas*) is a strict carnivore with a host of special adaptations that help it hunt. Its long legs and suckers on each digit allow it to climb with ease. Its feet are partially webbed, making it a good swimmer. It has excellent eyesight to home in on prey. It can even subtly change its body color to blend in with its surroundings. In fact, despite all appearances, this little frog is a fast, agile, and skillful predator.

ACTUAL SIZE

E WITH ITS BRIGHT green skin, red eyes, and orange feet, the tree frog is one of the most instantly recognizable of all rainforest animals. Unlike many rainforest species, the tree frog is not endangered itself, but its habitat is vanishing rapidly. About 80,000 acres of tropical rainforest are cut down every day to make way for farms, roads, and more homes for humans. With all its exotic beauty, the red-eyed tree frog is a living reminder of just what the planet stands to lose if we continue to destroy the natural world. In fact, this little frog has become something of a pin-up for rainforest conservation.

Where in the world?

Red-eyed tree frogs prefer habitats that are close to water, which they need to breed. They are found in American rainforests from southern Mexico to northern Colombia. They are also popular pets.

Did you know?

● In nature, animals that carry poison for self-defense often have colorful bodies. These warning colors deter predators. It is such a successful strategy that some harmless animals have evolved to mimic the appearance of more dangerous species. For instance, although the red-eyed tree frog resembles members of the poison dart frog family, it isn't poisonous.

● During the breeding season, the female tree frog lays her eggs on a leaf above a pond. Once hatched, the newborn tadpoles fall into the water below. At this stage they look more like fish than frogs.

● Male red-eyed tree frogs can grow up to 2in (5cm) long. Females are generally a little larger, at up to 3in (7.5cm).

● Tree frog tadpoles feed on fruit flies and pinhead crickets. Adults are also primarily insectivores (insect eaters), but have also been known to eat smaller frogs.

PHOTOFILE: Red-eyed Tree Frog

ᴱ **Warning!**
When a tree frog is in danger, it flashes its blue flanks and opens its eyes. These warning colors startle any potential attackers, giving the lithe and agile frog time to jump to safety.

FACT

Immature tree frogs are usually dark brown; they gradually turn green as they grow to adulthood. During their tadpole stage, they can change color, like a chameleon. By day, they are green and at night they turn a red-brown, which helps make them less conspicuous. Adult red-eyed tree frogs seem to retain this ability and have been seen to alter their color slightly to better blend in with their environment.

G First discovery

Although rainforest tribes
have known about the red-eyed
tree frog for generations, it was
first scientifically described by
Edward Drinker Cope (1840–1897)
in 1862. Cope was a noted fossil
hunter and herpetologist (someone
who studies amphibians).

E Gripping suckers

Wide suckers on the toes help the frog to grip
onto branches. By day, the frogs use these
suckers to attach themselves to the underside
of a leaf where they can sleep in safety.

Vine Snake

Scientific Name: Genus *Oxybelis*

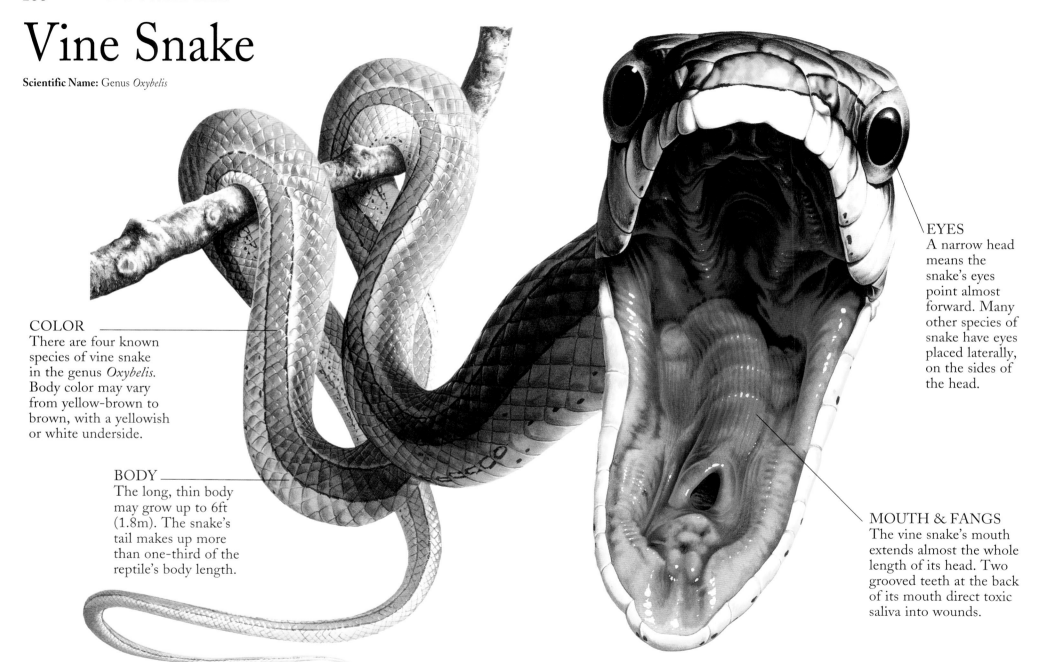

COLOR
There are four known species of vine snake in the genus *Oxybelis*. Body color may vary from yellow-brown to brown, with a yellowish or white underside.

BODY
The long, thin body may grow up to 6ft (1.8m). The snake's tail makes up more than one-third of the reptile's body length.

EYES
A narrow head means the snake's eyes point almost forward. Many other species of snake have eyes placed laterally, on the sides of the head.

MOUTH & FANGS
The vine snake's mouth extends almost the whole length of its head. Two grooved teeth at the back of its mouth direct toxic saliva into wounds.

Skilled at both the slow, silent hunt and the sudden, darting attack, the vine snake (genus *Oxybelis*) is one of the rainforest's most underrated predators. With its long, slender shape and tree-colored body, it easily blends in with its surroundings. This camouflage allows it to get within inches of prey before lunging forward to make a kill. While many species of snakes flick their tongue rapidly in and out of their mouth, vine snakes hold their tongue outside the mouth and move it slowly. No one

ACTUAL SIZE

knows for certain why, but some scientists think the snake uses its tongue as a lure, in the same way as a fisherman putting a worm on a hook. Once it has made a catch, few animals escape that gaping mouth!

E VINE SNAKES ARE diurnal, meaning that they are most active during the day. Many snakes have eyes on either side of their head. However, as the vine snake has such a narrow head, the reptile's eyes are much closer together, giving it binocular vision. From its vantage point high in the trees, this snake can spot ground-dwelling prey, such as lizards and amphibians, without being seen itself. When it does, it reacts quickly and silently. Slithering down the tree trunk, it gets as close as it can to its prey. Binocular vision allows it to judge distances very accurately so it strikes with great precision.

Where in the world?

Vine snakes range from the southern United States to South America as far as Peru. The Roatan snake is a native of Roatan Island. Generally, green vine snakes inhabit rainforests. Browner species live in savannahs and dry forests.

Did you know?

• When it is in danger, the Mexican vine snake is known to release a foul-smelling liquid.

• It has been reported that when it attacks large prey, the vine snake will bite into its victim's head and hold it off the ground to stop its prey from struggling.

• There are four known species of vines snakes in the genus *Oxybelis*: Cope's vine snake, the green vine snake, the Mexican vine snake, and the Roatan vine snake.

• The Roatan vine snake was only discovered in 1995. There may be many more snake species still to be discovered.

• Green vine snakes are such fast and skillful predators that they can catch hummingbirds! The snakes position themselves near flowers and strike when the birds come close to feed.

PHOTOFILE: Vine Snake

ᴇ **Vine disguise**
The Mexican vine snake's long body is no thicker than a pencil, making it easy to mistake one for a genuine rainforest vine. In fact, these snakes are difficult to spot in their natural habit unless they move.

FACT

Although *Oxybelis* vine snakes look similar to whip snakes of the genus *Ahaetulla*, they are not related. The similarity is due to convergent evolution. This occurs when different species develop similar physical characteristics. *Oxybelis* vine snakes and *Ahaetulla* whip snakes live in similar habitats so they evolved similar physical traits. Similarly, although birds, insects, and bats live in different environments, they all developed wings because flight is a useful trait.

G Grooved fangs
Snakes' fangs are either
hollow or grooved. The vine
snake has grooved fangs, similar
to some species of poisonous lizards.
The snake's fangs are positioned
toward the back of the mouth.

E Mexican vine snake
The Mexican vine snake can grow up to
6ft 2in (1.9m) in length. Due to its coloration
it is also known as the brown vine snake.
Oxybelis wilsoni is golden-yellow; other
species are yellow-green.

Western Diamondback Rattlesnake

Scientific Name: *Crotalus atrox*

TAIL & RATTLE
The tail is covered in black and white stripes and ends in a rattle. The rattle is made from the same substance as hair and nails (keratin).

SIZE
The largest diamondback grows up to 6ft 6in (2m) long and can weigh up to 11lb (5kg). The adult males are much larger than females.

HEAD & BODY
The western diamondback rattlesnake is easy to recognize, with its bulky body, large, triangular head, and rows of diamond-shaped patterns running along its back.

FANGS
When the rattlesnake bites down on its prey, muscles squeeze the venom glands and poison is forced out and into the snake's hollow fangs.

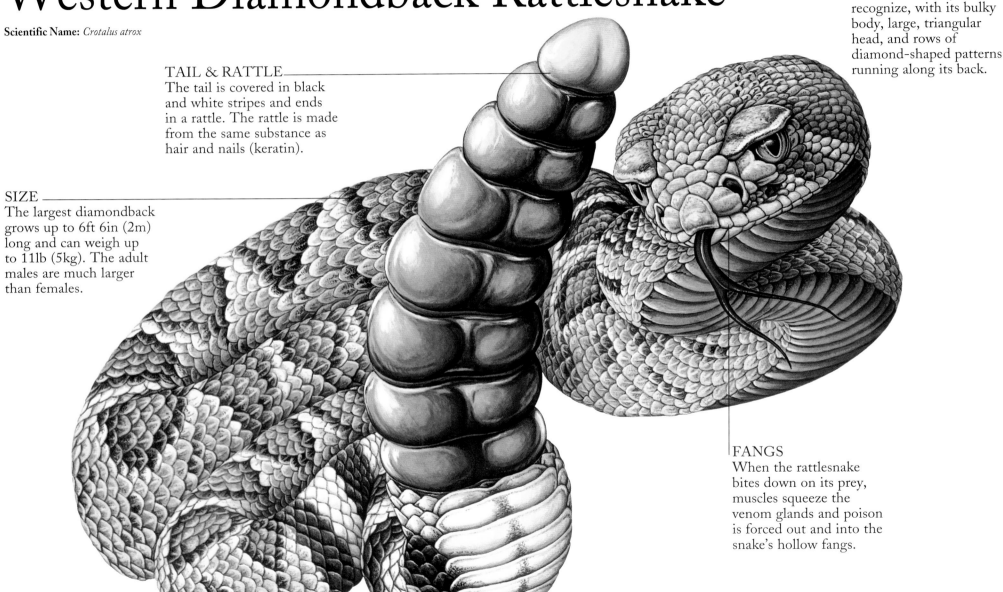

The scary rattle of the western diamondback rattlesnake (*Crotalus atrox*) is one of America's most terrifying sounds. This creature is as deadly as it is beautiful. The diamondback is a pit viper and uses sensitive pit organs to detect body heat. These organs are so acute that, even blind, a snake can target specific parts of its victim. Once it is close enough to strike, long, retractable fangs spring forward. The fangs are hollow, allowing poison to be injected directly into the prey's body.

ACTUAL SIZE

This venom destroys tissue, causes internal bleeding, and ultimately leads to death. Even if the prey manages to get away before the poison takes effect, it will be lucky to escape its ultimate fate in the rattlesnake's belly!

E THE WESTERN diamondback rattlesnake's most distinctive feature—its rattle—is used for defense rather than offense. When alarmed, the snake will hiss loudly and shake its rattle to warn intruders to stay well away, but that doesn't always work! This wolf is curious rather than aggressive. Edging closer, it sticks its snout down for a sniff. Big mistake! The snake lashes out, defending itself the only way it knows. The bite could easily kill but if the wolf is lucky the snake may not waste poison on something it can't eat, and just "dry bite," injecting little or no toxin.

Where in the world?

Diamondbacks are found from California to the Gulf of Mexico. They prefer dry regions, but inhabit any area where prey is plentiful. They are a terrestrial (ground-dwelling) species and especially prey on reptiles and burrowing mammals.

Did you know?

• Diamondbacks live up to 30 years in captivity, and up to 20 in the wild.

• Rattlesnake mothers give birth to as many as 25 young.

• A rattlesnake can shake its rattle over 60 times a second for up to three hours at a time!

• The rattle grows along with the snake. Extra segments are added to the rattle every time the snake sheds its skin. However, the size of the rattle can't really be used to tell the snake's age as they may shed their skins up to four times a year.

• Snakes don't have movable eyelids. Instead their eyes are protected by a transparent layer (a brille), which restricts eye movement. As they have eyes on either side of their head, though, they have a wider field of vision than humans.

PHOTOFILE: Western Diamondback Rattlesnake

E **Biting snake**
Rattlesnakes can control the amount of poison they inject. About 25 percent of bites on humans are "dry bites," but an angry snake will not only use a lot of venom, it may bite several times!

FACT

Every year, an average of 15 people in the United States die from snake bites. The country has around 20 poisonous snakes; the western diamondback and its eastern relative are the species responsible for most of these fatalities. More people are bitten by the American copperhead, but their bite is less toxic and the species is more likely to be found close to human habitation, where medical help is readily available.

G Males and females
It is difficult to tell male and female rattlesnakes apart because there is no variation in color and usually no difference in size between males and females. However, the male usually has a longer tail.

E Snaky scales
Snakes are covered in rows of scales that protect their bodies from damage and dehydration. The scales on the top and sides of the snake's body are smaller and thinner than those on the snake's underbelly.

Leatherback Turtle

Scientific Name: *Dermochelys coriacea*

CARAPACE
Most turtles have an outer shell protecting their body. The leatherback is unique because its upper body is covered by thick skin containing osteoderms (bony deposits).

FLIPPERS
The leatherback's front flippers can grow up to an incredible 8ft 10in (2.7m) in length. These are used to propel the turtle through the water.

BODY
Seven ridges run along the turtle's back. These make the leatherback's body more hydrodynamic, which helps it to move through the water more easily.

MOUTH
The leatherback doesn't have teeth. Instead, its beak (known as the tomium) has sharp, cutting edges. Backward-facing spines in its throat help the turtle to swallow food.

The leatherback turtle (*Dermochelys coriacea*) is the only remaining member of a family whose ancestors once shared Earth with the dinosaurs. This huge sea turtle is an impressive creature. On land, it is slow, sluggish, and vulnerable, yet in the ocean it's transformed into a swift and graceful hunter. A leatherback can weigh as much as 1,500lb (680kg), and a body that size needs a lot of fuel. It preys on species like the lion's mane jellyfish, which are plentiful because other animals wouldn't dream of eating them! This jelly's trailing tentacles are packed with stinging cells, but this doesn't seem to bother the turtle. In fact, it consumes around 73 percent of its body weight every day in jellyfish.

ACTUAL SIZE

▷ ALTHOUGH SHE SPENDS most of her life at sea, this female leatherback returns to the beach on which she was born to lay her eggs. Once there, she hauls her huge body above the waterline where, under cover of darkness, she starts digging. Using her huge flippers like a shovel, the turtle digs a hole in which she lays up to 100 eggs at a time. After she has covered her eggs with sand, the mother turtle returns to the sea. The temperature inside the nest determines the sex of the baby. Higher temperatures produce females; cooler temperatures produce males.

Where in the world?

Leatherback turtles were once one of the most widespread species of reptiles. Today they can be found in the Atlantic, Indian, and Pacific oceans, as far north as Norway and as far south as New Zealand.

Did you know?

● After they are born, male turtles spend their whole lives at sea. Females only set foot (or rather flipper) on land to lay their eggs.

● In 2008, one leatherback turtle was tracked migrating more than 12,000 miles (19,312 km) from its feeding grounds to its nesting site. Only the Arctic tern travels further, with one tern notching up a record-breaking migration of 50,000 miles (80,467km).

● When hunting, leatherbacks have been known to dive to depths of 4,200ft (1,280m).

● The turtle's mouth is the perfect tool for handling tricky food like jellyfish. Its sharp lip is used to grasp prey, while backward-pointing spines in its mouth and throat stop their slippery food from escaping.

● Leatherbacks often mistake plastic bags for jellyfish. These can kill the turtle if eaten.

PHOTOFILE: Leatherback Turtle

▷ **Big flippers**
Not surprisingly, the world's biggest turtle also has the largest flippers of any turtle. They are also the largest turtle flippers in proportion to body size, with a span of 8ft 10in (2.7m).

FACT

Mammals use food as fuel to warm their bodies. Reptiles warm their bodies by basking in the sun. This means that they struggle to survive in extreme temperatures, especially the cold. Leatherback turtles can tolerate the cold much better than other reptiles thanks to layers of fat under their leathery skin, which insulates them from the chilly waters of the North Sea. They also have a specialized circulatory system that helps to reduce heat loss.

△ **Fast swimmer**
According to *The Guinness Book of World Records* (1992), the leatherback turtle is the world's fastest-moving reptile. Swimming at top speeds, these huge beasts can reach a staggering 22mph (35km/h).

▷ **Hatchlings in danger**
After a two-month incubation, the turtle eggs hatch and the newborns make a dash for the sea. It is a dangerous time, as the hatchlings are vulnerable to predators both on land and in the ocean.

American Copperhead Snake

Scientific Name: *Agkistrodon contortrix*

TAIL
Young copperhead snakes have a yellow or green tip at the end of their tail. This tip turns dark brown as they grow older.

FANGS
Generally, the longer a snake is, the longer its fangs are. The hollow fangs of the American copperhead can be ¼in (6mm) long. This allows venom to be injected directly into their prey. Each snake has up to seven pairs of replacement fangs in their gums.

PITS
All pit vipers have a pair of deep pits between their eyes and nostrils. These are the external openings for a pair of sensitive detecting organs.

The American copperhead snake (a pit viper) (*Agkistrodon contortrix*) lies in ambush. Hiding under fallen leaves, the viper is almost invisible, which it uses to its advantage. The snake strikes only when its prey is almost on top of it. Ordinarily, the copperhead's fangs are folded back inside its mouth, but as its jaws open, its fangs spring forward and lock into position. The snake's poison is haemolytic—it causes veins to lose their ability to contain blood. This helps to break down the animal's body ready to be eaten. When attacking large prey, the copperhead bites then releases its victim to give the venom time to take effect. Smaller prey is usually held in the snake's mouth until it dies.

ACTUAL SIZE

▷ MOST SNAKES ACTIVELY avoid trouble, but when the American copperhead senses danger it "freezes," relying on its camouflage to hide it until the threat has gone away. Unfortunately for this snake, this long-distance truck driver has just got out of his cab to stretch his legs in exactly the wrong place. Fear takes over and the man picks up a stick and tries to beat the snake to death. The snake is terrified and fighting for its life. It lunges forward and plunges his fangs deep into the man's face. The bite is unlikely to be fatal, but it will be painful!

Where in the world?

Five species of copperhead are known: broad-banded copperhead, northern copperhead, Osage copperhead, southern copperhead, and Trans-Pecos copperhead. Each species inhabits a different region and different habitats, from southeastern America to the Gulf of Mexico.

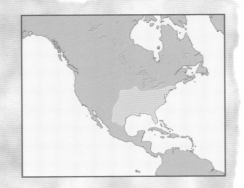

Did you know?

● Young copperheads use their green-tipped tails as a lure to attract reptiles and amphibians. They will also eat insects, which they actively pursue.

● The venom of the southern copperhead snake contains contortrostatin. In medical trials, it has been found that this protein stops the growth of cancer cells.

● Copperheads hibernate during the winter, using a communal den that they share with timber rattlesnakes and black rat snakes.

● The venom of a newborn copperhead snake is just as toxic as the venom of the adult.

● Sometimes when a copperhead is touched, it gives off a scent that smells a bit like cucumbers!

PHOTOFILE: American Copperhead Snake

▷ **Heat sensors**
The larger hole between the snake's eye and nose is the opening for its heat-sensing pit organ. An organ on both sides of head allows the snake to judge the distance and direction of its prey.

FACT

Just how does a snake eat an animal that is larger than its own head? The answer lies in the reptile's unusual anatomy. Most predators have strong jaws held together by powerful muscles, but snakes' jaws are joined by flexible ligaments. This allows them to open their jaws by as much as 180°. The skull bones are only loosely joined together too, so, as the snake stretches its mouth over its prey, its skull "flexes" to make room.

△ **Copperhead coloring**
Rather than broad bands,
the northern copperhead has
hourglass-shaped stripes running
along the length of its body.
Juvenile snakes are light brown in
color but turn a darker, chestnut
brown as they grow.

▷ **Broad-banded copperhead**
Its scientific name, *Agkistrodon contortrix
laticinctus*, is a bit of a mouthful, but to residents
of the southern United States this striped snake
is known as the broad-banded copperhead. The
color of the bands varies from region to region.

Gaboon Viper

Scientific Name: *Bitis gabonica*

HORNS
This species is easily identified by the pair of "horns" visible between the snake's nostrils. These vary in size in the two subspecies.

BODY
Members of the viper family are typically short and thick in the body, with a wide head to accommodate their large venom glands and long fangs.

FANGS
All poisonous snakes have venom glands, along with two pairs of specialized teeth (either hollow or grooved) that are used to inject prey with venom.

HEAD
The Gaboon viper's pale, leaf-shaped head makes a striking contrast to its beautiful geometrically patterned body. These patterns are known as "cryptic camouflage."

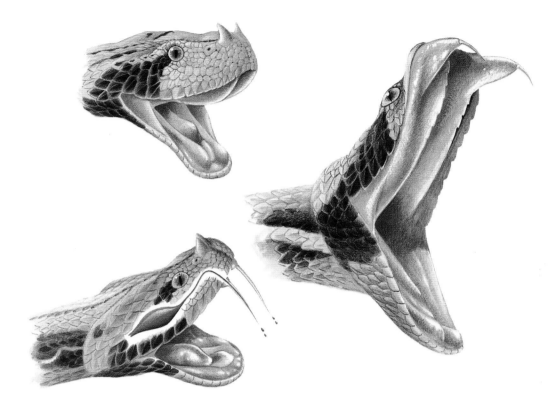

Gaboon vipers (*Bitis gabonica*) are super-sized snakes, growing up to 6ft 6in (2m) in length. Like all members of the genus *Bitis*, these snakes are heavy, with thickset bodies, a short tail, and a wide, oversized head. Inside that big head is a set of massive fangs. The Gaboon viper has the world's longest fangs; these allow it to inject massive quantities of venom very quickly. Most vipers will bite large animals, then allow them to crawl away to die before they track them

down to eat them. This prevents the snake from being injured as its prey struggles. However, the Gaboon viper is muscular enough to hang onto its prey, which can be as big as a monkey or a small antelope.

ACTUAL SIZE

▷ INSIDE THIS LARGE HEAD are the viper's massive fangs. The Gaboon viper has the longest fangs of any snake, growing up to 2in (5cm) in length. At rest, the snake's fangs lie flat against the roof of its mouth, protected by a fine membrane sheath. Once prey is in sight, the viper opens its mouth fully. This allows the snake's fangs to swing forward into position to bite. The viper's venom glands are enormous. In fact, the Gaboon viper produces the largest quantity of venom per bite of any poisonous snake. Bites on humans are rare, but can be deadly.

Where in the world?

In common with many members of this deadly snake family, the Gaboon viper makes its home in central, sub-Saharan Africa. They are at their most at comfortable among trees and foliage in rainforests and in plantations.

Did you know?

• Gaboon vipers are considered to be one of the most placid species of venomous snake. They will even allow themselves to be handled without biting their handler—although this is not advisable!

• Although they are called vipers, they do not have the heat-sensing pit organs that members of the Crotalinae group of snakes, such as the South American rattlesnake, have.

• Snakes are very adaptable reptiles. Some have even taken to the air! The flying snakes of southeast Asia don't have wings, but, by flattening their body and rippling their muscles, they can glide from treetop to treetop. In fact, they are technically better gliders than flying squirrels.

• Gaboon vipers are viviparous, which means that the females give birth to live young rather than laying eggs.

PHOTOFILE: Gaboon Viper

▷ **Deadly bite**
Despite its placid nature, Gaboon vipers have one of the fastest and most deadly bites of any snake. When threatened, it will rear up, reveal its fangs, and hiss to warn off any attackers.

FACT

This beautiful snake has a very distinctive pair of "rostral horns" between its raised nostrils. These tend to develop as the snake grows and can become fairly prominent. Despite their name, these horns aren't horns at all. Real horns are made of bone covered in keratin, which is the same material found in nails and hair. Rostral horns are made from scaled protuberances. They are common features in lizards as well as other species of snake.

△ **Folding fangs**

The snake's mouth must open by nearly 180 degrees to allow the fangs to spring into position. When not in use, the fangs fold back against the roof of its mouth, covered by a protective membrane.

▷ **Leaf camouflage**

The Gaboon viper's camouflage is a superb example of adaptive evolution. Even the snake's head is shaped and colored like a leaf, allowing it to lie, almost completely invisibly, among leaves and vines on the rainforest floor.

Mugger Crocodile

Scientific Name: *Crocodylus palustris*

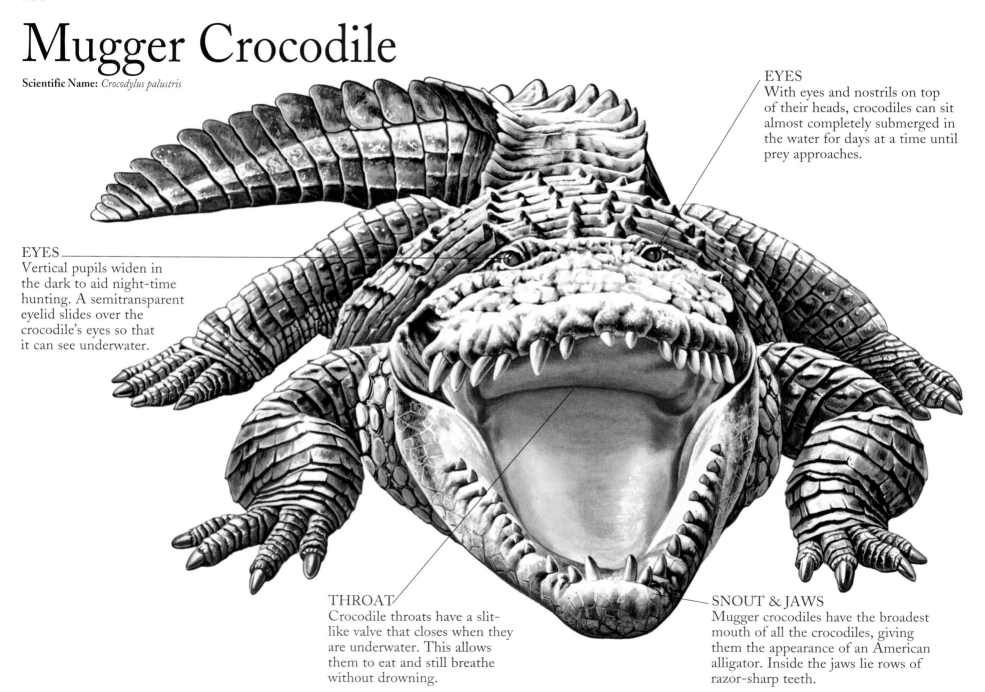

EYES
With eyes and nostrils on top of their heads, crocodiles can sit almost completely submerged in the water for days at a time until prey approaches.

EYES
Vertical pupils widen in the dark to aid night-time hunting. A semitransparent eyelid slides over the crocodile's eyes so that it can see underwater.

THROAT
Crocodile throats have a slit-like valve that closes when they are underwater. This allows them to eat and still breathe without drowning.

SNOUT & JAWS
Mugger crocodiles have the broadest mouth of all the crocodiles, giving them the appearance of an American alligator. Inside the jaws lie rows of razor-sharp teeth.

Anything that comes near the water to drink is fair game for the mugger crocodile (*Crocodylus palustris*). Although it will happily hunt fish, the mugger is easily capable of grabbing an animal the size of a deer from the riverbank and dragging it into the water with its powerful jaws. As crocodiles cannot chew, they drown large animals and store their bodies in underwater larders until they begin to rot, which makes it easier to tear the carcass apart. This powerful reptile has fantastic eyesight, powerful jaws, and can swim at almost 8mph (13km/h). It will even hunt on land, lying in wait near well-used forest trails for prey to pass by. All of these factors makes them amazingly efficient hunters.

ACTUAL SIZE

▷ FEEDING LAZILY in the shallow water, this Asian open-billed stork has no idea that death lurks just a few feet away. Half-submerged in the water, the mugger crocodile looks more like a piece of driftwood than a dangerous predator. The mugger is in no hurry, taking its time to edge ever closer to the stork. Then, just as the bird is about to fly off in alarm, the crocodile attacks. With surprising speed, it lunges at its prey with its red, gaping mouth flung wide open. The stork has no chance of escape, and the mugger finally gets the meal it has waited so patiently for.

Where in the world?

These fearsome crocodiles are found throughout the Indian subcontinent. They are a freshwater species and prefer slow-moving water. They can be found in manmade canals and reservoirs as well as rivers and marshy areas.

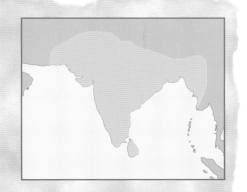

Did you know?

● Muggers belong to a group of reptiles called crocodilians. The crocodilians' closest living relatives are birds!

● The name mugger means "water monster."

● Crocodilians are an ancient group of reptiles that were so successful as a species that they have changed very little since dinosaurs ruled the Earth over 83 million years ago.

● The largest-known mugger crocodile measured 17ft (5.2m) in length. It is thought that they may grow even larger with age.

● Crocodilians may be killers, but they are dedicated parents. Unusually in the reptile kingdom, both parents take part in rearing the young.

PHOTOFILE: Mugger Crocodile

▷ **Waterproofing**
The mugger crocodile's ears are covered by a movable flap of skin that closes when the animal is underwater. The eyes and nostrils can also be closed to stop waters from getting in.

FACT

How can you tell the difference between an alligator and a crocodile? Alligators have rounded, U-shaped snouts, with broad jaws that are designed for cracking bones and breaking open turtle shells. Crocodiles have longer, more pointed, V-shaped snouts with weaker jaws that are adapted to a more varied diet. The mugger crocodile is unusual because it has a broad, fairly flat snout. This makes it look more like an alligator than a crocodile.

△ Strong swimmer
As you might expect, muggers
are superb swimmers. However,
although they have webbed feet,
they don't use them for swimming.
Instead, they propel themselves
through the water using broad
sweeps of their flat, muscular tail.

▷ Mugger's teeth
Inside the mugger's mouth are 66–68 teeth. It is
these that help distinguish them from alligators. The
mugger's teeth are perfectly aligned and the large,
visible fourth tooth proves that it is a true crocodile.

Glossary

Agile—moves quickly and easily

Binocular vision—sight using both eyes to cover the same field of vision. An animal with binocular vision, such as a human, has a better idea of how far away objects are.

Camouflage—colors, patterns, or body shapes that allow animals to blend into their surroundings

Carcass—the body of a dead animal

Carnivore—an animal that only eats meat

Crustacean—an arthropod with a toughened outer shell covering its body, such as a crab

Dormant—in a state of rest similar to sleep

Endangered—where there is a risk of a species dying out

Evolution—the process of changing and adapting to an environment over time

Extinction—when the last remaining member of a species has died

Habitat—area where an animal or plant normally lives

Hibernation—a time when some animals become less active in order to conserve energy. They slow down the speed at which they breathe, lower their body temperature, and survive on stored fat.

Immune—protected from

Incubation—to keep eggs warm until ready to hatch

Juvenile—young, not adult

Ligament—a band of tough tissue that connects bones or supports muscles or organs

Mammal—a warm-blooded animal with fur or hair on its skin and a skeleton inside its body. For example, elephants, dogs, cows, and humans.

Membrane—a thin layer of tissue that covers or lines parts of the body

Marsupial—mammals, such as kangaroos, where a female has a pouch to carry her young in

Migrating—traveling over long distances looking for food sources or nesting sites when the seasons change

Nocturnal—active at night

Order—a related group of living things. Snakes and turtles both belong to the reptile order.

Paralyze—to be unable to move

Plumage—the feathers of a bird

Prey—the animal that is hunted by a predator

Retractable—can be pulled back

Rodent—a small mammal, such as a mouse, with long front teeth for gnawing

Savannah—a flat grassland in tropical or subtropical regions

Solitary—alone

Species—group of animals or plants that look and act very like each other. Members of the same species can breed together.

Stamina—the ability to remain active for a long time

Streamlined—a shape that has the least resistance to wind or water.

Subtropical—in a region immediately to the north or south of the tropical zone

Talon—a sharp claw, especially that of a bird

Tropical—a region around the Earth's equator, where the weather is warm all year round

Venom—a type of poison

Index